DATE			

The East–West Pendulum

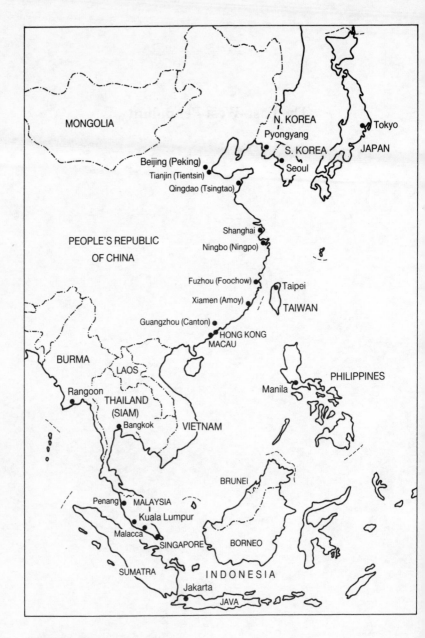

Figure 0.1. The Asia–Pacific region

THE
EAST–WEST
PENDULUM

*A risk–reward analysis of Asia
to the year 2000*

Robert Lloyd George

Q

Quorum Books
New York · Westport, Connecticut

Published in the United States and Canada by Quorum Books,
an imprint of Greenwood Publishing Group, Inc.

English language edition, except the United States and Canada,
published by Woodhead-Faulkner (Publishers) Limited.

First published 1992

Library of Congress Cataloging-in-Publication Data

Lloyd George, Robert.
 The East-West pendulum / Robert Lloyd George.
  p.   cm.
 Includes bibliographical references and index.
 ISBN 0-89930-778-7 (alk. paper)
  1. East Asia–Economic conditions.   2. Asia, Southeastern–
Economic conditions.   3. Capital market–East Asia.   4. Capital
market–Asia, Southeastern.   I. Title.
HC460.5.G46   1992
330.9–dc20   91-47949
                                                            CIP

© Robert Lloyd George 1992

Library of Congress Catalog Card Number: 91–47949

ISBN 0-89930-778-7

Printed in Great Britain

For
My Mother

China – there lies a sleeping giant. Let him sleep, for when he wakes, he will shake the world . . ..   Napoleon

But nothing of [the conflicts of British party politics] counted much against the great movements in history. None of our struggles mattered much, wars or revolutions or what you will, as compared with the sheer biological and geographical facts. Whatever happened, in two hundred years, perhaps sooner, the balance of the world would have changed. The industrialisation of Russia was taking place: India would follow: perhaps China, within a hundred years.

Whatever Governments presided over the operations, these changes would make our local concerns look no more significant than the War of the Roses.
David Lloyd George, quoted by C. P. Snow,
Variety of Men

Trade with the Far East was only possible thanks to exports of gold and silver, ...

So during the sixteenth and seventeenth centuries there circulated throughout the vast Asian continent, source of spices, drugs, and silk, the precious gold and above all silver coins minted at Venice, Genoa or Florence, and later the famous Spanish silver pieces of eight. Away to the East flowed these currencies, out of the Mediterranean circuit into which it had often required so much patience to introduce them. The Mediterranean as a whole operated as a machine for accumulating precious metals, of which, be it said, it could never have enough. It hoarded them only to lose them all to India, China and the East Indies. The great discoveries may have revolutionised routes and prices, but they did not alter this fundamental situation, no doubt because it was still a major advantage to westerners to have access to the precious merchandise of the East, in particular pepper, which according to one Venetian 'brings with it all the other spices . . .'; no doubt also because in the sixteenth century, as in the past, the purchasing power of precious metals rose above that of Christian countries as soon as one crossed the border into the Orient.

Fernand Braudel,
The Mediterranean in the Age of Philip II

Oh East is East, and West is West, and never the Twain
    shall meet
Till Earth and Sky stand presently at God's great
    judgement seat
But there is neither East nor West, Border nor Breed,
    nor Birth
When two strong men stand face to face, though they
    come from the Ends of the Earth.

Rudyard Kipling

The balance-sheet of cultural influence is overwhelmingly one-sided. The world gave back to Europe occasional fashions, but no ideas or institutions of comparable effect to those Europe gave to the world . . .. For centuries, thousands of European ships sailed to Calicut, Nagasaki and Canton. During those same centuries, not one Indian, Japanese or Chinese ship ever docked at Tilbury, Genoa or Amsterdam.

J. M. Roberts
A History of the World

CONTENTS

LIST OF FIGURES AND TABLES

FIGURES

TABLES

PREFACE

In ancient times Chinese people explained the nature of the world as a basic dualism. Yang is male, light, hot, active; yin is female, dark, cold, passive. Unlike the dualism of the Mediterranean world, in which good and evil are in perpetual conflict, yin and yang are mutually complementary and balancing. The greater yang grows, the sooner it will yield to yin; the sun at noon is starting to give way to night. The interdependence of the two principles is well symbolized by an interlocking figure which today is used as the central element in the flag of the Republic of Korea. Actually, the yin–yang concept often seems more useful than Western dualism for analyzing nature and also human affairs. It neatly fits the rhythms of day and night, summer and winter, and the balancing roles of male and female.

This dualism may also be applied to East and West. The East has, for the past one thousand years or more, had a great preponderance in terms of the numbers of humanity, of economic resources and of continuous civilization. Why did the Chinese Empire recover from the early barbarian incursions of the early fourth century when its contemporary in the West, the Roman Empire, collapsed and declined into the Dark Ages? On the other hand, the question may be asked, why did China never have an age of exploration and science such as the West's Renaissance, the Age of Enlightenment? Despite Western supremacy in the field of ideas, it was only from 1800 onwards that Western traders and colonial powers managed to dominate the Asian peoples.

The argument of this book is that Asia is once again on the move and that during the next ten years it will again be the centre of the world economy. It has already replaced the United States as the locomotive of the world economy with its new spending power, its new technology and its growing capital resources. Within Asia the leadership is changing too. Japan has led the wave of modernization since the Second World War. It has led in management and in technology and has maintained a stable political system. Now, however, it is the overseas Chinese states of South East Asia which are taking up the baton. My contention is that the leadership of Asia, in economic and cultural terms, will pass to the Chinese during the next twenty years.

There are sound arguments for this prediction. The first is the proven genius of the Chinese race throughout the past three thousand years of continuous civilization. The accomplishments of the Chinese people in the field of scientific and technological invention as described by Joseph Needham in his book *Science and Civilisation in China*, are a further proof of the creativity and artistic brilliance exhibited in Chinese painting, ceramics and literature. For example, the great surviving monuments of the early Ming Dynasty, the Forbidden City and the Temple of Heaven in Peking, may be compared with the remarkable construction of the Chinese city states of Singapore and Hong Kong in the past thirty years. An age of large-scale building activity reflects the underlying confidence of the culture. As we approach the year 2000 it is clear that the centre of gravity in the Chinese world has moved south. Historically it was centred on the Yellow River and laterly the Yangtse, typically on the cities of Xian, Nanking, Peking and Shanghai (from 1850 to 1950). Today the centre of economic and, increasingly, cultural activity is the Pearl River and the coastal city of Hong Kong, which may be described as the nerve centre of the overseas Chinese world.

If we imagine Hong Kong as the focal point of a number of concentric circles which encompass Taiwan, Guangdong Province in the inner circle, Singapore, Malaysia, Thailand, Indonesia and the Philippines, with their important Chinese communities in the second circle, and then further flung cities such as Vancouver, San Francisco, Sydney and perhaps London in the outer circle, it becomes apparent that the fate of Hong Kong after 1997 will have a ripple effect far beyond the city itself. The dynamic part of the Asian world is in the hands of these overseas Chinese communities. Anything which damages their confidence will damage the growth potential of the region as a whole. The extraordinary economic growth of the past thirty years in the region is also a result of the fact that the genius of the Chinese people has been progressively liberated in this period following the colonial handover in Singapore, for example, and in the new economic freedoms which have characterized the boom in Taiwan and Hong Kong. Hence the importance in China itself today of the democracy movement and the progressive shift towards economic reform which will also liberate this entrepreneurial energy. 'Let the Chinese dragon sleep . . .' (Napoleon).

My purpose in writing this book is to attempt to analyze risks and rewards for investors in Asia today based upon an historical analysis of each country. In particular, political stability is judged by experiences of the past, and the Asian response to foreign investors today is judged by the pattern of response a century ago to Westerners.

The chapters in this book fall into four groups. Chapters 1, 2 and 3 discuss Asian economic history. Chapters 4 and 5 deal with risk reward analysis, and Chapter 5 in particular describes a risk reward analysis for each of the Asian countries concerned in this book. Chapter 6 looks at the emerging capital markets within Asia, and finally Chapter 7 makes forecasts for Asia to the year 2000.

This book is intended for the general reader and for students who may wish to learn more about the region which is likely to have most impact on their lives in the next fifty years. It may also, I hope, be useful for businesspeople thinking about investment in the Asia–Pacific region. As an investment manager myself much of my thinking has naturally been devoted to the analysis of economies and capital markets. However, in the course of the ten years I have lived in Asia, it has become very apparent to me that without understanding the culture, traditions and beliefs behind the economic statistics we cannot possibly hope to make informed investment decisions. This book, therefore, is a modest attempt to try to fill that gap of understanding and to communicate my enthusiasm about the region to the reader.

ACKNOWLEDGEMENTS

This book owes its concept to a number of people. First, I would like to mention Antony Norman who first showed me a book written in 1895 by his father, Henry Norman, *The People and Politics of the Far East* (Norman, 1895). This splendid book inspired me to think for the first time of trying to write a sequel nearly a century later. Secondly, I would like to thank Sidney Frankel who asked me to give a talk with the title, 'Has the world gone East?', and this did a great deal to clarify my thinking about the historical movement which I am trying to describe. In addition, it was due to the warm and enthusiastic response that I have received from audiences in Europe and North America when I have given presentations about the Asian markets, and the many questions which I have received on Japan, China, Hong Kong and its future after 1997, Thailand and the other developing countries of Asia.

During the four years I have been researching and preparing this book, I have conducted a great many interviews with leading political and academic figures and businesspeople throughout Asia and I would like to take the opportunity here to thank them all for their time and encouragement. In Hong Kong, Lord Kadoorie, Sir Roger Lobo, Helmut Sohmen, William Purves, Hari Harilela, Martin Lee, T. S. Lo, Gordon Wu, Donald Tsang, Professor T. L. Tsim, Professor Edward Chen, Derek Davies and Frank Ching. In Korea, Chang Soon Yoo, Yong-Shik Kim, Professor Euh Yoon-Dae, Tai Ho Lee, C. Ferris Miller and Professor Sung Tae Ro. In Japan, Hisao Kanamori, Nobuyuki Arai, and Hiromitsu Takemi. In Taiwan, Dr. Chang Rong-Feng, Dr Chuang-Lin and Dr Hwang Yueh Chin. In China, Xu Ben Hao, Jing Shuping, Liu Yi Min, Professor Gong Hao Cheng and Zhang Xiaobin. In Indonesia, Marzuki Usman and Suyanto Gondokosumo. In Malaysia, Kamal Saleh and Khatijah Ahmed. In Singapore, Toh Chin Chye. In Thailand, Dr Olarn Chaipravat and Dr Maruay. In Canada, David Lam. In Australia, Malcolm Fraser, Professor Jeffrey Blayney and Helen Sham Ho, MP.

I would like to acknowledge various authors from whom I have quoted including *Science and Civilisation in China* by Joseph Needham (Needham and Ronan, 1978, 1981, 1986). *The East–West Pendulum* owes its final appearance to the unfailing support and encouragement of Sally Rodwell both in Hong Kong and in Cambridge. I would also like to thank my old friend Philip Snow who undertook a painstaking process of correcting my Chinese history, names, dates and facts. Many of the statistical tables I owe to the hard work and research effort of Scobie Ward and Caesar Luk. And finally my sincere thanks to Pamela Raggett.

1

INTRODUCTION TO THE EAST-WEST PENDULUM

The best prophet of the Future is the Past

(Byron)

He was called 'Il Milione' – the man who talks in millions. He had come back from the East with fabulous, incredible tales of wealth and splendour. Even his own family turned him away from the house, until he opened his dirty, travel-stained cloak, and poured out emeralds, rubies and sapphires onto the table. His name was Marco Polo, and he was the first Westerner to visit China and also to attempt to describe (in 1295) its geography, government, economic life, culture and technology which were manifestly so much more advanced than early Medieval Europe.

'Il Milione' became, in the Middle Ages, a byword for the incredible. Yet modern knowledge of China has vindicated the Venetian story teller. His 'black stones' mined from mountains, for example, proved to be coal. Even his detailed itineraries of Central Asia have been verified. And his perception of the strength, wealth and longevity of Chinese civilization was profound. From the thirteenth to the nineteenth century China maintained its position as the most powerful and unified world power. The thesis of this book is to examine how and why the pendulum of history which has swung so visibly and decisively towards the West in the past two hundred years is now beginning to return at an accelerating pace toward a twenty-first century world dominated by the East, in wealth, in population, in technology and in economic dynamism.

THE EAST–WEST INDEX

The East–West index is intended to be a composite relative indicator of economic and technological progress. One of the main factors is the flow of capital between East and West which, before 1840, comprised a regular flow of silver from Europe to China (see Figure 1.1). By contrast, in the last thirty years there has been a steady annual trade deficit between the United States

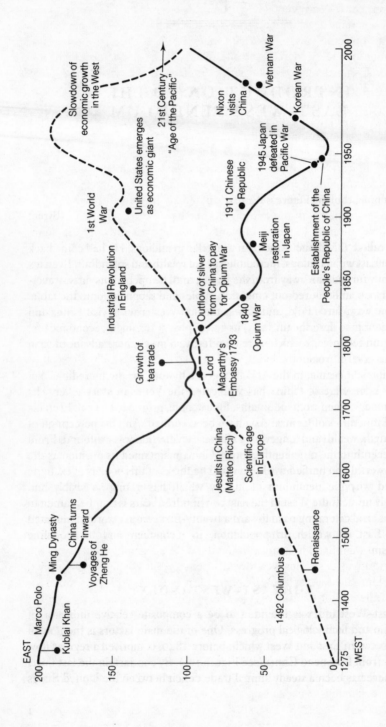

Figure 1.1. The East-West index (A composite relative indicator of economic and technological progress – per capita GNP, scientific knowledge, military strength, geographical discoveries – comparing China and Europe and including, from 1850 onwards, United States and Japan)

EAST

200

Kublai Khan
Marco Polo
Ming Dynasty
Voyages of Zheng He
China turns inward

150

Growth of tea trade
Industrial Revolution in England
1st World War
United States emerges as economic giant
Slowdown of economic growth in the West

Jesuits in China (Matteo Ricci)
Scientific age in Europe

100

Lord Macarthy's Embassy 1793
Outflow of silver from China to pay for Opium War
1840 Opium War
Meiji restoration in Japan
1911 Chinese Republic
United States emerges as economic giant
21st Century "Age of the Pacific"

50

1492 Columbus
Renaissance
1945 Japan defeated in Pacific War
Establishment of the People's Republic of China
Korean War
Nixon visits China
Vietnam War

0

WEST

1275   1400   1500   1600   1700   1800   1850   1900   1950   2000

and Japan. For the early centuries, of course, we do not have exact figures for levels of economic development, gross national product (GNP) or population. We can, however, make educated guesses, based on the first-hand observations made by Marco Polo and others, of the standard of living and culture in China compared with Europe. The historian Fernand Braudel, in his books *The Mediterranean* and *Civilisation and Capitalism*, did attempt to quantify these economic differences, notably by using price levels in different areas of the world during the Middle Ages (Braudel, 1972 and 1984). Thus, the author has used many different sources to reach actual historical comparisons. The overall index is bound to overweight certain factors at different times. What may be called the psychological factor in the development of certain civilizations at certain times is considered important. For example, the confidence of the early period of the Ming Dynasty, 1380 to 1450, is contrasted with the faltering leadership of the later Qing Dynasty, from 1800 onwards, which in turn may be compared with the expanding confidence of the British Empire at the same period.

Also included in the East–West index is the relative per capita GNP in West and East. For instance, Hong Kong's average personal income is now about US $12,000 and it is expected to overtake that of the United Kingdom in the next few years just as Japan's per capita income, aided by a strong yen, overtook that of the United States in 1989.

Scientific discoveries and inventions and the level of national technology are an important part of the index. Before 1400 China was technologically in advance of the West and Marco Polo's astonishment at many aspects of life in China under the rule of Kublai Khan attests to this contrast. Gunpowder, paper money, printing, the quality of silk apparel, the sophistication of the culinary art, the skill in navigation and many other examples can be cited. Table 1.1, which appears later in this chapter, details Chinese inventions and discoveries and the time which elapsed before many of these ideas reached the West or were independently discovered in the West.

Allied to applied technology is, of course, the important factor of military power. The Chinese discovered gunpowder but did not use it for military purposes and this may be a major reason why China was consistently defeated by Western military expeditions during the nineteenth century. Skill in navigation went hand in hand with the thirst for geographical discovery and the curiosity or desire for wealth which impelled it. China's great admiral, Zheng He, sailed as far as Arabia and East Africa in the 1420s, but 1433 marked the end of China's overseas expeditions. By contrast, Christopher Columbus' voyage across the Atlantic in 1492 marked the beginning of a long period of exploration and discovery by Western navigators. No greater contrast can be found between the two mentalities. Just as China closed in on itself during the later Ming period and early Manchu Dynasty, so the West was accelerating its momentum in the age of scientific discovery, reformation and the beginnings of capitalism in Europe.

Many scholars consider that equality between China and Europe ended in 1793 on the occasion of the British Ambassador, Lord Macartney's, visit to the Emperor Qian Long at his summer palace. From this time on there was a steep decline in China's relative power and influence. After 1860 calculating the Asian balance becomes more complex since at that point the rapidly modernizing Japan comes into the equation. From the Meiji restoration (1868) onwards, Japan moved at extraordinary speed to strengthen its economy, its military and naval capability, and its technological potential. However, the West was also strengthened by the emergence of the United States as a great power around 1900. The turning point of Asian power and influence may be considered (again symbolically) as 1950. Firstly, because European colonial powers retreated from South East Asia. Secondly, the end of the US military occupation of Japan and the Korean War marked the beginning of the economic boom in Japan, while Mao Zi Dong's proclamation in Peking on 1 October 1949 that 'China has stood up' was perhaps the single most important event. China's confidence had been restored and, whether under communism or under a freer system in the overseas Chinese communities, the Chinese would begin a generation of tremendous economic advance after one hundred years of impoverishment, corrupt regimes and domination by the Western colonial powers.

The growth of Asia in the past forty years has been astonishing and it has included both communist nations such as China, as well as Japan and the other free Asian nations. China, under the communists, moved rapidly to solve the age-old problem of famine. A strong, unified central state was re-established, and this maintained a strong People's Liberation Army. In this respect, the organization of the country was akin to the early years of previous dynasties.

None the less, the pendulum of history has been visibly swinging back towards Asia in the past forty years. The most obvious indicator is economic growth which has averaged 7 per cent per annum in Asia during the past four decades as compared with 3 per cent in Western countries. The continuation of this trend is the basis for my forecast that Asian economies will account for more than 50 per cent of the world's economic production before the end of this century. The equation is simple. The rapid growth in population, multiplied by the growth in personal income, equals an economic boom. It also promotes political stability. Modern communications have done much to underpin this economic boom. The Boeing 747, the telephone and the fax machine have shrunk the Pacific and accelerated trade flows, between Japan and California, Hong Kong and Canada and many other countries.

My prediction, therefore, that the East–West pendulum in the twenty-first century will be swinging firmly towards Asia should not be viewed by Western readers with alarm. It is, perhaps, the most positive event at this stage of the world's history because it will spread the new wealth of Asia throughout the globe, increase not only the supply of Asia's goods but also the demand for Western goods and services. Our knowledge and appreciation of Asian culture may also grow and the potential gain for the world economy and living standards in the poorer developing countries will be enhanced. Economic growth, therefore, will not be confined to Asia, but will spread its positive effects towards Australia, the Western half of the United States and Canada and eventually to the European Community where many Asian manufacturers have begun to establish factories to supply European consumers.

ASIAN RELIGIONS AND PHILOSOPHIES

Western readers who think of Asia as the home of mysticism are often surprised to discover that Asians are in many ways rather more materialistic than Westerners. It is important, therefore, to look at the roots of Asian beliefs. In East Asia, that is China, Japan and Korea, Confucianism had a greater and more powerful influence than subsequent religions such as Buddhism, Islam or Christianity. The societies of China and Japan are based on the tenets of Confucius which advocate order, respect, hierarchy, good manners and the sacrifice of the individual for the greater good of the family or the community. It is often said that the secret of the amazing corporate success of Japan and Korea lies in the strong Confucian work ethic. As always, the truth is probably more complex but undoubtedly the ideas of Confucius continue to play an important part in the life of ordinary people in East Asia and they foster the strong sense of family, the respect for age and seniority and the high savings rate.

Buddhism has a strong influence in countries such as Thailand and also, to a lesser extent, in Japan. However, the pragmatic and worldly approach which allows a Japanese to be baptized in the Buddhist faith, to be married according to Shinto and to be buried according to the Buddhist rites also allows a Buddhist monk in Bangkok to play the Thai stockmarket on a daily basis. These are some of the paradoxes of life in Asia.

Christianity has never taken a very firm hold in East Asia, apart from in Korea. At the height of the missionary effort in the eighteenth century it is estimated that no more than 1 per cent of the Chinese population was converted. About 1 per cent of the Japanese population today professes Christianity. By contrast, more than 25 per cent of South Koreans are practising Christians and this has had an important influence in the political life of that country. In the Philippines the church plays a very important role in politics and Mrs. Aquino's rise to power in 1986 owed much to the support of Cardinal Sin.

The Judaeo-Christian tradition of the West puts great value on each human life, whereas in the Asian tradition the life of the community, the corporation and the family is of greater importance. Many things flow from this difference.

The emphasis on human rights and democracy is one. Asians feel less concerned about the niceties of democratic procedure. Social harmony and consensus is usually of paramount importance. Individual initiative and individual creativity is of less importance than the willingness to merge one's personal identity in the life of the company (in Japan) or of the family (in Chinese societies). Perhaps this is why there are fewer Nobel prize winners in Japan than in the United States. The opposite side of the coin is the example of the many refugees in Hong Kong and elsewhere in South East Asia who have personally sacrificed so much to build up their family businesses and educate their children, working eighteen hours a day over decades to achieve it.

In the middle, both geographically and philosophically, stands Islam. When Zheng He sailed around the Indian Ocean and visited East Africa his guides were Muslims. When Marco Polo visited China, again his guides were Muslims. In the Middle Ages the Muslims were always the go-betweens between East and West.

In China today there are estimated to be 50 million Muslims. When the great monolithic blocs of communism in the Soviet Union and China finally crumble, this central Asian world will return to its natural state and the Muslim population will become of great strategic importance, straddling as it does the borders of the Soviet Union and China. Hence recent events in the Middle East have stirred fears not only in Moscow but also in Peking. Asia is home to more than half of the world's Muslims. There are 180 million in Indonesia, perhaps another 100 million in India, 90 million in Bangladesh and 100 million in Pakistan. Until only recently it was considered that the large Muslim populations of Malaysia and Indonesia were relatively pragmatic, worldly and less fundamentalist than their brethren in the Arab world. However, the rise of OPEC and its great wealth, the overthrow of the Shah by the Ayatollah Khomeini and the rising tide of fundamentalism throughout the Arab world has had its effects on the Muslims of Asia. In Malaysia, Umno, the ruling party which in the past tried to hold the balance between the Malays, the Indians and the Chinese, has now increasingly to take into account the aspirations of the fundamentalist groups. In Indonesia, too, for the past twenty-five years Suharto has managed to contain this rising tide. When he retires some time in the 1990s (or dies) it may be much more difficult to restrain this movement from gaining greater political influence. This will have major consequences for the wealthy and influential Chinese minority in Indonesia. Muslim minorities are also restive in the Philippines. So Islam has a political and strategic impact in many places in Asia and it still stands, as it has done in past centuries, as a buffer between East and West, between Christianity and Confucianism.

Before turning from the impact of religion on Asian society, it is appropriate to consider the spiritual and moral vacuum manifest among the younger generation in China since the collapse of Marxist ideology and the exposure of Maoism as a hollow creed. More and more young people in China are turning to the underground churches which have sprung up, especially in the south, and this may well be a pointer to the future. However, in general the hunger of the young and growing Asian populations is for material goods and it is likely that even if a religious revival sweeps through the world in the late 1990s, Asians will remain pragmatic and more committed to bettering their standard of living. This will certainly be the foundation of political stability in Asia and it will enable those countries with ethnically diverse communities, such as Malaysia and Indonesia, to satisfy the aspirations of their growing populations without internal conflict. Therefore much, but not all, depends on economic development. However, the religious and philosophical traditions on which the Asian boom is based should not be ignored as they will continue to influence the character and durability of that boom as it spreads more widely into the Pacific region.

ASIAN TECHNOLOGY AND ECONOMIES

An important part of the East–West composite indicator is how technology and the impact of scientific inventions have affected people's every-day lives both in China and, latterly, in Japan as compared with the West. Marco Polo was impressed by the smooth organization of life under Kublai Khan and the arrangements for transport, money, food and clothing, agriculture and engineering. Table 1.1 demonstrates this clearly in the way it highlights the long time gap (on average 1400 years) between basic inventions in China, which were made in the Han Dynasty or earlier, and their belated arrival in Europe in the late Middle Ages or the Renaissance. However, another table could be made characterizing the past five hundred years as being the lag time before the Chinese, and latterly the Japanese, adopted the new science of the West including medicine, transport and military technology.

Today it is the semiconductor which is the key to so many inventions and so much economic development. Japan has established a clear lead over the United States in this key technology.

Asian nations now possess almost all the technology possessed by the West and this is a major cause of their drawing level in the economic field. The fact that the United States and the Soviet Union have been locked into a high-spending arms race for the past thirty years has actually benefited Japan, which has been able to devote a much higher percentage of its GNP to peaceful civilian research and development. Japanese, Korean and Taiwanese companies have concentrated on producing not what the Pentagon ordered, but what the consumer wanted. This is the main reason for their commercial success and their financial strength today. Shifts in the world balance of power in the late 1980s may possibly influence the Japanese to spend more on their

Table 1.1. Chinese inventions and discoveries and time lags before recognition or adoption in the West

Discovery/invention	Year discovered	Years before adoption in the West
Agriculture		
Row cultivation of crops and intensive hoeing	600 BC	2,200
The iron plough	600 BC	2,200
Efficient horse harness – trace	400 BC	500
– collar	300 BC	1,000
The rotary winnowing fan	200 BC	2,000
The multi-tube (modern) seed drill	200 BC	1,800
Astronomy and cartography		
Recognition of sunspots as solar phenomena	400 BC	2,000
Quantitative cartography	200 AD	1,300
Discovery of the solar wind	600 AD	1,400
The Mercator map-projection	1000 AD	600
(Mounted) Equatorial astronomical instruments	1300 AD	600
Engineering		
Spouting bowls and standing waves	500 BC	never
Cast iron	400 BC	1,700
The double-acting piston bellows – air/liquid	400 BC	1,900/2,100
The crank handle	200 BC	1,100
The 'Cardan suspension', or gimbals	200 BC	1,100
Manufacture of steel from cast iron	200 BC	2,000
Deep drilling for natural gas	100 BC	1,900
The belt drive (or driving-belt)	100 BC	1,400
		1,800 (significantly realized in West)
Water power	100 AD	1,200
The chain pump	100 AD	1,400
The suspension bridge	100 AD	1,800
		(possibly over 2,200)
The first cybernetic machine	300 AD	1,600
		(possibly 3,000)
Essentials of the steam engine	500 AD	1,200
'Magic mirrors'	500 AD	1,500
		(before understood in West)
The 'Siemens' steel process	500 AD	1,300
The segmental arch bridge	610 AD	500
The chain-drive	976 AD	800
Underwater salvage operations	1100 AD	800
Domestic and industrial technology		
Lacquer, the first plastic	1300 BC	3,200
Strong beer (sake)	1100 BC	never
Petroleum and natural gas as fuel	400 BC	2,300
Paper	200 BC	1,400
The wheelbarrow	100 BC	1,300
Sliding calipers	100 BC	1,700

Table 1.1. (Contd)

Discovery/invention	Year discovered	Years before adoption in the West
The magic lantern	200 AD	1,800
The fishing reel	300 AD	1,400
The stirrup	300 AD	300
Porcelain	300 AD	1,700
Biological pest control	300 AD	1,600
The umbrella	400 AD	1,200
Matches	577 AD	1,000
Chess	600 AD	500
Brandy and whisky	700 AD	500
The mechanical clock	725 AD	585
Printing – block printing	800 AD	700
– movable type	1045 AD	400
Playing-cards	900 AD	500
Paper money	900 AD	850
'Permanent' lamps	900 AD	never
The spinning-wheel	1100 AD	200
Medicine and health		
Circulation of the blood	600 BC	1,800
Circadian rhythms in the human body	200 BC	2,150
The science of endocrinology	200 BC	2,100
Deficiency diseases	300 BC	1,600
Diabetes discovered by urine analysis	700 AD	1,000

Source: Science and Civilization in China

military, but common sense and the experience of the past forty years might suggest to them that they have a unique economic advantage by not doing so. In his influential book *The Japan That Can Say No*, Ishihara argues that Japan really holds the balance since it alone can produce the integrated circuits which are incorporated into all ballistic missiles, whether American or Russian (Ishihara, 1991).

Technology then will be one of the keys to protecting Asia's success in the 1990s and thereafter. It will no longer be simply a question of copying Western inventions and improving on them. We can expect to see scientific breakthroughs from the Japanese, not least in areas such as biotechnology.

Turning to Asian economies, Figure 1.2 looks at the Chinese economy in the nineteenth century. It illustrates the sharp downturn in China's trade figures during the 1830s resulting from the British strategy of selling opium to the Chinese to pay for the growing export of tea, which had been costing Britain up to 5 million ounces of silver in the early 1820s. As the volume and value of opium imports grew rapidly during these years so China's trade slipped into deficit.

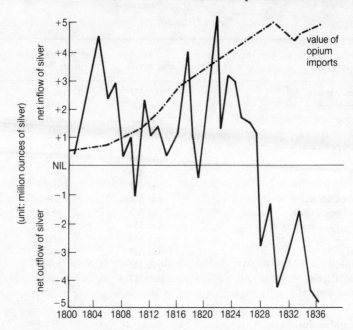

Figure 1.2. The Chinese economy in the nineteenth century – China's silver payments go into deficit

The trade relationship between the United States and Japan in the past forty years (as shown in Figure 1.3) provides a mirror image of that of Britain

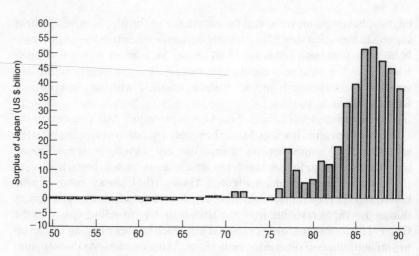

Figure 1.3. Trade figures between United States and Japan, 1950–1990

and China a century earlier. During the 1950s and 1960s there was little that America wanted to buy from Japan, and Japan ran a steady but small annual trade deficit with the United States. It is worth remembering that, in the immediate aftermath of its defeat in the Pacific War in 1945, it was thought by most American economists that Japan would remain a purely agricultural producer and have little or no industry to speak of. It was at exactly this time of post-war privation and hardship that new and dynamic small businesses sprang up in the suburbs of Tokyo and Osaka under the brand names of Sony, Honda, Matsushita, Sharp and Nissan. Above all, it was the car manufacturers who were responsible for the dramatic change in the United States–Japan trade balance beginning in the late 1970s. In his book, *The Reckoning*, David Halberstam compares the story of Nissan Motor with Ford (Halberstam, 1987). The heavy built, unattractive, slow and unmarketable models which Nissan first brought to the United States in 1962 and which were scoffed at by American manufacturers were transformed ten years later, into competitive and attractive models which rapidly increased their share of the huge American automobile market during the energy-conscious decade of the late 1970s and early 1980s. Added to the tremendous growth in car exports were televisions, transistor radios, videotape recorders, computers, semiconductors and even less technological items such as golf clubs.

The peak of Japan's export success was in 1987 when the trade surplus with the United States reached US $52 billion. The shift in purchasing power and wealth had already occurred at the time of the 'Plaza Accord' in September 1985, which effectively revalued the yen against the dollar by 50 per cent from Y250 to Y120. No other single measure of Japan's economic success can compare. Overnight per capita income levels in Japan soared to the equivalent of US $24,000 per head, higher than the average American income. The size of the Tokyo stockmarket also soared past that of the New York Stock Exchange in terms of capitalization. The Japanese started buying properties in New York, Los Angeles, Hawaii, London and even bought long-established English golf courses and old French vineyards. Perhaps the most striking, single example of their new-found wealth was the extraordinary prices they were prepared to pay for Impressionist paintings, especially Van Goghs, during the late 1980s.

An important question to ask now is whether Japan's 'supremacy trend' has peaked or is Japan experiencing a temporary dip in a long-term trend which may endure another twenty years? Hazardous as it is to make such a forecast, the resilience and economic strength of Japan today is such that not even an earthquake in Tokyo of the scale of the great 1923 Kanto quake would disturb this long-term trend. Although the momentum of growth in Japan will slow down, the international diversification of its investments will produce a steady growth in its overseas income, more than enough to offset a slowdown in export sales. Japan will still be the chief provider of credit and investment to the Asian region. Thus, it will play a central role in the expected growth of South East Asia and China in the next twenty years, mainly as banker and investor to developing Asian countries such as Thailand, Indonesia, Malaysia and the Philippines.

2

THE ROOTS OF CHINESE CULTURE

BACKGROUND TO CHINESE CULTURE

In this chapter I will attempt to summarize some key points about China and the Chinese to provide the background for my analysis of Chinese economic history, China's response to the West, the success of today's overseas Chinese and their underlying business culture.

Traditionally, the family rather than the individual, or the state, has formed the basic unit in Chinese society. In China the rule of law is of less importance than in the United States and Europe where conflicting elements in a society such as church and state, capital and labour, government and business, are balanced by the law. By contrast, in traditional China personal virtues of loyalty and honesty, sincerity and benevolence, backed up by the family system provided the basis for commercial contact. Law was a necessary tool of administration but personal family relationships were the foundation of society. Many of the problems of modernization in Chinese society today result from this aspect of Chinese culture.

From early times the Chinese have considered the unity of the state of prime importance. Unaware of the great cultures of the West they considered China the centre of civilization surrounded on all sides by barbarians. They called their country *Zhongguo*, literally the 'central country' commonly translated as the 'Middle Kingdom'. Zhongguo is still the Chinese name for their land. They looked down on all foreigners as being inferior and uncivilized and many of the problems of early diplomatic contacts with the West stemmed from this notion of the Middle Kingdom.

The Chinese writing system has linked many of the peoples of the Asian continent. All literate Chinese, even if they speak mutually unintelligible dialects, can read the same books and feel that written Chinese is their own language. The linguistic map of East Asia shows the full extent of the influence of China or rather the Sinitic languages. It does not clearly indicate, however, that both the Korean and Japanese languages, though very different in origin, borrowed their systems of writing from China and are thus culturally tied to China.

13

The teachings of Confucius (551 to 479 BC) still have a major influence on society in East Asia today. Confucius, like his Greek contemporaries, Plato and Socrates, was essentially a teacher of ethics. His main thesis was that good government was a matter of personal morality. He insisted that the first duty of a statesman was to set a proper example of sound ethical conduct. He argued that the rule of virtue and the contentment of the people, rather than power, should be the true measure of political success. His ideal ruler was a *Junzi* which is usually translated as 'the superior man' or 'gentleman'. He placed a great emphasis on ritual and etiquette and believed people should foster inner attitudes through the practice of external forms. He set the East Asian pattern of compromise, of seeking the middle path. His emphasis on moderation, balance and harmony has moulded the Asian psyche. Confucianism eventually became the accepted wisdom of successive generations of scholars and officials while the emphasis on learning and the establishment of the examination system opened the political arena to all people of talent from whatever social background.

During the past two thousand years of Chinese history a pattern is discernible of a new dynasty starting with a dynamic emperor asserting a vigorous rule over the empire and maintaining the unity of China, establishing a strong army, collecting the taxes and settling frontier disputes. Usually within one hundred years, according to the pattern, government begins to show a gradual deterioration. The decline starts with a failure to collect taxes and results in financial problems in the civil service and the army, with increasingly hostile tribes on the northern frontier of China. This was true of the Ming Dynasty. It was also true of the Qing Dynasty. The question is, how will the Communist Dynasty, which began in 1949 with Mao Zi Dong, reflect the pattern of China's dynastic history?

An historian will always hesitate before saying this is a new era, with a new set of factors. My contention is that China remains the same. The Cultural Revolution of 1966–76 was compared by the historian, Professor Trevor Roper, to the Boxer Rebellion of 1898–1900. In both cases the Western legation in Peking were besieged by huge crowds of students and soldiers waving anti-Western placards. The opening up of China during the 1980s may also be compared to the situation in the late-nineteenth century when China opened up to Western trade and missionaries for the last time, though only under the compulsion of superior Western military power. The pendulum swings back and forth between allowing Westerners in and expelling them – the yin and yang of the 'Middle-Kingdom' mentality and international awareness and openness. It may be argued that Deng Xiaoping's most decisive contribution to the future of China was his decision in 1979, following his visit to the United States, to send 50,000 of China's brightest and best young people to study in the West, mainly in America. One of the consequences of this decision was the upsurge of students peacefully demonstrating for democracy in Tiananmen Square in May 1989. My own belief is that in the longer term China will not again, in the next fifty years, turn in on itself since it now has a Western educated, internationally minded, young elite who will, in the normal course of events, be the rulers of China in the period 2000 to 2030.

But the dynastic pattern may well survive. In the 1980s we have seen that certain Chinese leaders – Deng Xiaoping, Zhao Ziyang, Yang Shangkun and his brother Yang Baibeng, and Ye Jianying – have each tried to place their children in influential positions in order to perpetuate the family's influence. On Deng Xiaoping's death the dynastic struggle will undoubtedly be a struggle between the leading families in Peking. The corruption, which has grown so rapidly in China during the economic boom of the 1980s, was also the result of the old Chinese tradition of ensuring favours for members of one's family. It will undoubtedly continue to be a characteristic of the way China does business with the outside world and it may well become, in the twenty-first century if not before, one of the leading causes of the downfall of this Communist Dynasty as it has been of previous dynasties. Finally, corruption and lack of moral integrity, will leave a vacuum of power at the heart of the empire. Communist rule in China, for this reason, may well not survive until the end of the century, or even until 1997.

CHINESE EMIGRATION

The first Chinese emigrants started to leave China before 1400 (although there is evidence of Chinese merchant shipping in the Indian Ocean as early as 900) and it is around this time that the first historical voyages of Chinese trading fleets are recorded. The longest and most famous series of seven expeditions headed by the great eunuch, Admiral Zheng He, between 1405 and 1433, reached as far as Zanzibar and the East African and Arabian coasts. Already at that date there was a well-established Chinese community on the west coast of Malaysia at Malacca. Malacca is of great symbolic historical importance as the meeting place of East and West for medieval trade and the exchange of ideas, including the spread of Islam into the East Indies. It served as the base for St. Francis Xavier's missionary voyages to the Philippines, Macao and Japan. It seems likely, therefore, that the majority of Chinese emigrants going to the *Nanyang* or South Seas would have passed this way, through Malacca, and into both Malaysia and Indonesia. Some of the contemporary population of Singapore are descendants of the so called *Baba* Chinese of Malacca. Some of the largest communities of overseas Chinese populations are those in Malaysia, Singapore and Indonesia. Burma and Thailand, sharing a border with China, would also have received direct migration overland.

The provinces of China from which most overseas Chinese today originate are Guangdong, centred on the City of Canton and the Pearl River estuary, and Fujian from which came the settlers of Taiwan, the Fujianese or Hokkien people. From Canton, apart from the Cantonese, there were minorities such as the Hakka, and Chiu Chow who in the nineteenth century were mainly 'coolies' from the area around the port of Swatow (Shantou). Among today's Chinese population in Bangkok the majority are Chiu Chow. They are renowned for their skill in rice trading and banking and famous among the Chiu Chow community are the Soponpanich family of Bangkok Bank (originally surnamed Chin). Another celebrated Chiu Chow is Li Ka Shing, Hong Kong's leading real estate entrepreneur and one of the world's twenty-five richest men. The Hakka were a thrifty, hardworking, mountain people from the north eastern part of Guangdong Province (originally from Northern China) who moved not only to Hong Kong but also to Malaysia and Indonesia. The Fujianese or those who speak the Hokkien dialect predominate in the population of Singapore.

Mention should also be made of the smaller but highly influential community of Shanghainese people who emigrated in the 1940s, some to Hong Kong but others to Taiwan and the United States. They have been especially successful in the textile, shipping and banking fields and included in their number are leading businessmen such as Sir Y. K. Pao. Many United States Chinese businessmen, scholars and scientists are also Shanghainese in origin, such as An Wang of Wang Laboratories, the architect I. M. Pei and a number of Nobel prize-winning physicists.

It may seem surprising that none of the interior provinces of China and very few of the Northern provinces around Peking and in Manchuria provided any (or at least very few) of the Chinese emigrant population. Part of the answer seems to be that population pressure in the south was greater and so encouraged emigration. But it is also true to say that the grip of Mandarin culture and bureaucracy was less strong among the group of the southern Chinese who were and are more motivated towards trade than towards scholarship and the ideas of the Western world.

It is important to appreciate the subtle differences between these different overseas Chinese communities since these differences persist so strongly in present day business relationships and practices. In describing the dialects – Cantonese, Hakka, Chiu Chow, Fukianese, Shanghainese – for example, it should not be forgotten that most educated Chinese also speak Mandarin. In Taiwan, particularly, Mandarin is widely spoken although the local dialect is closer to that of Fujian province. In Singapore, also, the government has made strenuous efforts to promote the use of Mandarin as well as English as a national language. However, in the many Chinese restaurants in North America and Europe the language mainly spoken is Cantonese. The Cantonese are some of the most dynamic emigrants, the entrepreneurs and traders of the Chinese world. Nowhere can this be seen more clearly than in

Hong Kong, where the population is 98 per cent Cantonese, but this is equally true of Canton, and the other towns on the Pearl River estuary, which are much closer in spirit to Hong Kong than to other provinces in China. The common bond is the Cantonese language and the Cantonese people who are famous not only for their cuisine, but also for their energy and skill in commerce.

From Figure 2.1 it can be seen that the main destinations of the Chinese emigrants in the period 1860–1930 were Singapore and Malaysia, Thailand and Burma (mainly arriving overland), Indonesia and the Philippines. The settlement of Chinese traders in South East Asia alone pre-dates Western colonialism. The main influx started in the nineteenth century stemming from the local demand for coolie labour and the breakdown of order in China following the Tai Ping rebellion in the 1850s. Today, the overseas Chinese in these countries mostly stand on the periphery of politics but at the core of business life. There are exceptions to this rule, however, particularly in the Philippines and Thailand where assimilation has been greatest.

If we look at the size of the Chinese population in each country it is, of course, largest in Singapore, accounting for 77 per cent, and the only country where the government is dominated by the Chinese under the Confucian authoritarian rule of Lee Kwan Yew. In Malaysia, the Chinese are in a minority, accounting for 35 per cent of the population, compared with about 55 per cent of Malays. The Malays dominate the political scene and the Chinese dominate the business world. The minority is even smaller in the highly populated Indonesian archipelago where, out of 180 million people, only 3 per cent are Chinese. None the less, it is estimated that 80 per cent of the country's commerce is in the hands of the Chinese. In both Jakarta in 1966 and in Kuala Lumpur in 1969, there were fierce anti-Chinese riots and pogroms, so that the insecurity of the Chinese minority population is founded on events well within living memory.

The story is very different in Thailand, which, being predominantly Buddhist, is a tolerant and easy-going country which has assimilated its Chinese population as it has other foreigners. In fact, because of this long-established policy of assimilation, it is almost impossible to ascertain who is Chinese. A rough estimate would be that the Chinese community accounts for between 5 and 10 per cent of the total Thai population. Within Bangkok itself almost every major company, with notable exceptions such as Siam Cement, is dominated by Chinese management. Even more apparent are the strong interconnections of Chinese family businesses in these different countries, i.e. between branches of families in Bangkok and Hong Kong, between Taipei and Singapore, and between Jakarta and Kuala Lumpur. Most of the international trade in South East Asia, therefore, goes through Chinese trading companies and Chinese banks.

Another interesting case is that of the Philippines, to which there was also a

Figure 2.1. Chinese emigration in 1900

considerable amount of Chinese emigration in the late nineteenth century. There, too, the centre of economic power has shifted inexorably from the Spanish Mestizo (Spanish Malay elite) to the Filipino Chinese who, although accounting for only 3 per cent of the population, control as much as 60 per cent of the country's banking and commerce. The local Chinese are more racially exclusive than the native Filipinos. Their names are often unknown to other Filipino businesspeople and most of their foreign trade is conducted with relatives and clansmen in other countries.

In general, however, the tendency of the Chinese in the past has been to concentrate on business. Each family's experience of deprivation, starvation and refugee status from a communist regime is too recent to allow anything else. The tendency has been to do well for your family first and let others worry about political problems.

In the late 1980s, however, all this has begun to change rapidly. The ending of martial law in Taiwan in mid-1987 was symbolic not only of the eclipse of the Chiang family's power but of the emergence of a new democratic opposition. In Manila and Seoul the old authoritarian ideas have become rapidly outdated. The younger Chinese population is both more educated and more politically aware than their parents. Much of this might, perhaps, be traced to the influence of US university education on the younger generation in the past twenty years. It has, of course, had a profound effect on China itself where the decision of Deng Xiaoping, after 1979, not only to open China's doors to the world but, more importantly, to send China's best young people to study in Western universities, has proved to have had a more revolutionary effect than its architect had expected. It can be no accident that the Goddess of Democracy, which was erected in Tiananmen Square in May 1989, bears such a close resemblance to that icon of Jeffersonian ideals, the Statue of Liberty. There is no doubt that in the coming decade this political awareness and this new-found idealism in the Chinese younger generation will grow and become a more powerful factor throughout the Chinese world. Figure 2.2 shows Chinese emigration today.

In 1965 the United States took what proved to be an historic decision under President Lyndon Johnson. The Oriental Exclusion Act of 1884 which, for more than eighty years, had banned Chinese immigration into the United States was finally repealed and in its place the present quota system was set up. What this meant in practice was that for all Asian countries there would be a certain number of entrants allowed in automatically each year, excluding, of course, those with family ties and business immigrants. The demographic effect of this decision after more than twenty years can be seen clearly in the Table 2.1.

Compared with 1901–20 when 75 per cent of immigrants into the United States came from Europe and only 10 per cent from Asia, the early 1980s witnessed a shift to about 50 per cent from Asia and 20 per cent from Europe.

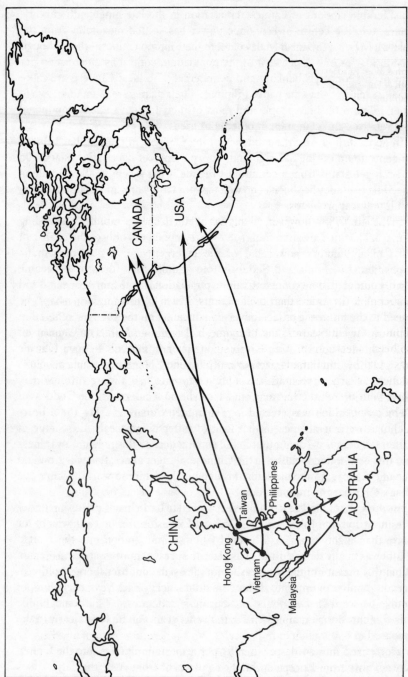

Figure 2.2. Chinese emigration today

Table 2.1 a) and b). Legal immigrants to the United States

a) Origin (%)	1900–1920	1981–1985	b) Location	Number
North & West Europe	34	6	New York City	97,510
South & East Europe	41	8	Los Angeles – Long Beach	64,453
North America	10	2	Miami – Hialeah	37,887
Asia	5	42	Chicago	20,297
Latin America	6	36	San Francisco	16,234
Others	4	6	Anaheim – Santa Ana, Calif.	12,998
			San Diego	12,706
			Houston	11,399
			San Jose	11,152

Note: These figures do not include the approximately 2.4 million illegal immigrants and illegal agricultural workers who will become legalized through the one-time amnesty programme in the new immigration law.

Source: 1986 Statistical Yearbook of the U.S. Immigration and Naturalization Service.

The balance of 30 per cent came mainly from Mexico and Latin America. The number of Asian Americans has climbed rapidly to exceed 6 million today. Of these, the largest ethnic groups, according to the United States census, are the Filipinos, the Chinese and the Vietnamese. A large number of refugees have also been taken in from Indo-China since the ending of the Vietnam War in 1975. Of the immigrants from the Philippines, Thailand, Malaysia and Indonesia, a large percentage are of Chinese origin. They also tend to be the people with the most education, skills and financial backing.

The numbers in themselves are, therefore, less important than the results of a highly motivated and educated group whose success, especially in business and in the academic world, has been out of all proportion to their size. It should be very clear, however, that the effect of this American policy change twenty years ago has been nothing but positive for the United States. What is very hard to measure is the total economic or cultural gain. Nobody knows how many dollars are invested in the United States each year from Taiwan, for example. Yet it is these invisible factors which have the greatest long-term impact.

Table 2.2 gives details of the 'Chinese diaspora', showing an approximate estimate of the size of the overseas Chinese populations around the world. A very conservative figure of 50 million has been reached which would represent about 5 per cent of the population of mainland China today, at 1.1 billion. This compares, for example, with an estimate of 11 million overseas Indians compared to 850 million in India itself. The Chinese, proportionately, have a far greater and more widespread influence, especially in South East Asia and increasingly on the western coast of Canada and the United States.

The case of Vancouver is especially interesting. The government of British

Table 2.2. The Chinese diaspora

	Population (million)
Taiwan	20.5
Hong Kong	5.7
Malaysia	5.5
Singapore	1.8
Indonesia	3.5
Thailand	4.0
Philippines	2.5
Other Asia	2.5
United States	1.5
Canada	0.5
Australia	0.1
United Kingdom	0.1
Others	0.5
Total (approx.)	50.0

Columbia has been very far-sighted and liberal in its policy approach. In the early 1980s there was high unemployment (about 15 to 20 per cent) in and around Vancouver. The British Columbian government took the courageous decision to allow in business immigrants especially from Hong Kong and latterly from Taiwan. This was facilitated by the fact that there had been a small Chinese community in Vancouver for over a century. The new influx in the 1980s brought a rapid rise in real estate prices as the 'yacht people'/ wealthy immigrants (to contrast them with the 'boat people' who arrive penniless in Hong Kong) arrived in large numbers to invest in property and seeking a safe haven from the political uncertainties of 1997.

No single person symbolizes this extraordinary social phenomenon more than Dr. David Lam. He came to Vancouver in 1966 with his family and soon set up a real estate company. Having made a large fortune, he proceeded to give much of his money away to good causes such as the university, the Baptist Church and Chinese community causes. In 1988 he was appointed Lieutenant Governor of British Columbia, becoming the most prominent overseas Chinese public figure anywhere. In fact, there is no parallel to his position among Chinese-American community leaders. Although many have excelled in business, few have become prominent in politics. In the United States the exception is probably Hawaii, where the Chinese population has long been involved in public life, but even there the Japanese Americans have provided more governors, senators and congressmen than the Chinese Americans.

THE CHINESE FAMILY

Neither the nation nor the company but the family is the basic unit of Chinese society. Just as if we want to understand the success of Japan we must study the Japanese corporation, so, too, to understand overseas Chinese business corporations, we must study the Chinese family. Apart from its economic importance there is also much that the West, with its high divorce rate, single-parent families and neglected senior citizens, can learn from the cultural and ethical traditions of the family in Chinese tradition.

The main ideas preached by Confucius were the principles of hierarchy, order and harmony within the society. The loyalty owed by a subject to the emperor parallels that owed by a son to his father. Chinese stories are full of examples of filial piety. A modern example of this is Frank Ching's excellent book, *Ancestors*, in which he traces the genealogy of the Ching family for one thousand years, back to a poet of the tenth century (Ching, 1988). He also recounts a number of moving stories of self-sacrifice illustrating this virtue of filial piety. To quote the philosopher Mencius, 'There are three ways of being an unfilial son. The worst is to have no heir.' In fact, so precisely did Confucius lay down the rules of social behaviour that each individual knew exactly his or her position within the family and, therefore, within society and his or her duty to each member of it. The hierarchy is based on generation, age, and sex.

Thus there are five human relationships in which human beings are involved, as follows:

1. emperor/subject,
2. father/son,
3. older brother/younger brother,
4. husband/wife, and
5. friend/friend.

Father/son relationships are central to the success of a continuing family business and this is still valid in overseas Chinese businesses today where it is rare for a son to take any important decisions while his father is alive. Nothing is more misleading than to be told that the family patriarch has 'retired'. (And this is equally true in the political arena, as we think of both Deng Xiaoping and Lee Kwan Yew, both formally, at least, 'retired'.)

The individual within the Chinese family is of far less importance than in the West. It is not the family which exists in order to support the individual but rather the individual that exists in order to continue the family. The reverse of Western thinking. For example, it is common that the brightest boy in the family, even if he is not the oldest, will be financed through college by the family on the clear, but unspoken, understanding that his subsequent lifetime earnings as a lawyer or a doctor, for instance, will be channelled back into the family's joint savings. A decision by the family to go into a certain kind of business, to buy a property or even to make an arranged marriage are all communal family decisions, taken together but ultimately obeying the wishes of the paterfamilias (but with proper respect for an ageing grandmother, for example).

Family and kinship relationships are very closely tied into overseas Chinese business activities. The family will not do business with people they do not know – no one deals with strangers. Business relationships are always, to some degree, personal relationships. Thus, business organization is built on the basis of kinship. A Hong Kong merchant would feel more comfortable in dealing with a second cousin living in Bangkok, for example, than in dealing with someone from a different area who lives next door to him. James Michener's story of the Yee family in his novel, *Hawaii*, provides a wonderful description of the Chinese family business (Michener, 1959).

The most essential asset in the Chinese business world is a good reputation. This may take years to acquire and can be lost very rapidly. In order to start a business one needs capital, of course, but that in itself is not enough. One must have *Xinyong* which means having a good reputation (and credit rating) with other members of the same profession. This is another reason why, in traditional China and in overseas Chinese communities today, legal contracts have been considered to be of little importance. In traditional China, the family have always come before the law. There is an almost universal Chinese aversion to lawsuits and arbitration. Personal relationships account for much more than contractual relationships. Threats to one's reputation, along with community sanctions, appear to have been sufficient incentives to act honourably and to maintain good faith.

If we try to sum up the style and essence of overseas Chinese business we can identify the following four characteristics:

1. Flexible decision-making by one strong individual.
2. Strong family control and connections to overseas cousins.
3. Highly informed financial planning (though unstructured in the Western sense).
4. Reliance on personal trust rather than legal contracts.

The importance of understanding Chinese business culture is underlined by the fact that much of the business of the Pacific Rim today is in the hands of overseas Chinese companies. Long before the large Japanese trading companies became so powerful, Chinese merchants and their family networks had already established an economic system throughout South East Asia. It would be impossible to prove statistically but it is estimated that 75 per cent of all trade in Indonesia, Malaysia, Singapore and the Philippines today goes through firms controlled by overseas Chinese.

Parallel to the view that the family is more important than the individual is the very different Chinese idea of time. Because the individual's life is of less importance, so a longer-term view can be taken of investment decisions, which may be meditated for many years. The most eloquent description of the individual's place in time is as follows:

Descent is a unity, a rope which began somewhere back in the remote past, and which stretches on to the infinite future. The rope at any one time may be thicker or thinner according to the number of strands (families) or fibres (male individuals) which exist, but so long as one fibre remains the rope is there. The fibres at any one point are not just fibres, they are the representatives of the rope as a whole. The living individual is the personification of all his forebears and of his descendants yet unborn. He exists by virtue of his ancestors, and his descendants exist only through him, the rope stretches from Infinity to Infinity passing over a razor which is the Present. If the rope is cut, both ends fall away from the middle and the rope is no more. If the man alive now dies without heir, the whole continuum of ancestors and unborn descendants dies with him (Baker, Hugh D. R., 1979).

There is a close link between this sense of family continuity and the importance of land in Chinese thinking. There is a continuous effort to secure wealth in the form of land. Land is very rarely sold. Most overseas Chinese people still have today a clear idea of the village from which their families originated. There is a strong pull back towards this motherland. The greatest virtue of land is its inherent illiquidity. The real advantage of land lies in its being difficult to sell in a hurry. Again, the emphasis is on the family's interest, not the individual's over a longer period of time.

Education is another basic element in Chinese family thinking. In traditional China, learning was the road to power and prestige which could be attained through competition in the civil service examinations. To be a scholar was to have an entry to the civil service and the power and security that went with official posts in Imperial China. In a sense, both land and education are linked to the Chinese search for security. Until very recently in many countries of South East Asia overseas Chinese were prohibited from owning land, therefore business skills and education replaced property ownership as the main route to wealth. The thirst for land and the thirst for education can both be traced to the insecurity which characterizes many overseas Chinese communities. Hong Kong is only one example and in Indonesia and Malaysia fear and discrimination motivate overseas Chinese to look around the Pacific Rim for suitable investment opportunities especially for real estate in North America.

THE FUTURE FOR THE CHINESE

Although I have tried to demonstrate the broad influence and power of this community of 50 million Chinese people living outside China, it is to China itself that we must return to understand the future influence of this region. In economic terms the 50 million of the Chinese diaspora have for the moment much more impact than the 1.1 billion people on the mainland but the challenge of that vast number remains.

Figure 2.3 shows that it is estimated that on current trends the population of China may stablilize at 1.5 billion by the year 2050. As Jing Shuping (President, China International Economic Consultants, Beijing) remarked, 'no country in the world has ever had to cope with the problems of economic development for such a large number of people'. (In fact, judged by results, the world's most successful economy is that of Taiwan which has a population of 20 million but, over a thirty year period, has averaged 8 to 10 per cent economic growth every year.)

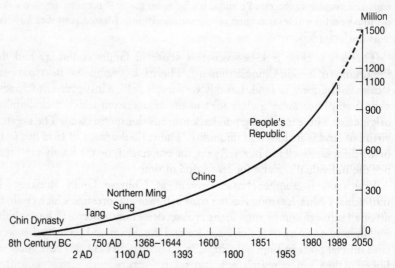

Figure 2.3. China's population

As yet the problems of this vast population have scarcely affected the rest of the world but it is not hard to imagine that even a small convulsion on the margin or, among the more educated members of the population, the search for new freedoms, could produce a large number of new refugees. In the past 150 years, the Taiping Rebellion, the Sino-Japanese war and the communist takeover in 1949 all had this consequence. As recently as 1962 a bad harvest and starvation in many parts of Southern China brought more than 100,000 people into Hong Kong. Hong Kong is, of course, suffering from the overflow of ethnic Chinese and other refugees from Vietnam in recent years. (There are now over 50,000 refugees from Vietnam in Hong Kong.)

The phenomenon of the boat people is not one which is likely to disappear in the near future. In fact, it is likely to get much worse in the 1990s as the failure of the communist system in both China and Vietnam produces a growing number of dissatisfied young people who will brave the risks of escaping by sea or land into a freer world. Just as Europe is now beginning to feel the effects of the Gorbachev revolution in the Soviet Union and Eastern Europe in terms of emigration, so too it may be that a small step towards liberalization in China and a greatly increased awareness of the outside world could produce a lot of people looking for a better life. The disappointment felt by many after the Tiananmen Square massacre in June 1989 has already left an estimated 50,000–100,000 People's Republic of China (PRC) Chinese citizens seeking political asylum or simply extending their stay in Western countries as well as Hong Kong.

In *The 2024 Report*, Norman Macrae and his son predict that when the world searches for a new model for economic development in the early twenty-first century the global competition will be won by an elderly Taiwanese professor who recommends the economic model of Taiwan in 1960–90, i.e. minimum government interference, low taxes, few regulations, and rapid two year product changes by small family-run companies (MacRae, 1984). In fact, this model was already being adopted in the late 1980s by many of the Chinese corporations situated along the coast, especially in Guangdong Province. The speed with which world export markets change today demands the kind of flexibility which is built into these small, family-run companies. It has been argued that the overseas Chinese are not, in fact, as successful at managing large, structured corporations as the Japanese and the Koreans. Typically the most successful Chinese businesses have been small, family firms. There is an inherent problem in the change of generations – very often the sons, though better educated than their fathers, do not have the same hunger and drive, and the growth rate of the company slows down. This phenomenon is familiar to experienced investors in South East Asia. However, more and more Chinese family companies are hiring professional managers in order to maintain the company's dynamism beyond the first generation.

3

DIFFERING RESPONSES TO THE WEST

In assessing the potential risk and reward for investors in each Asian country I believe there is probably no single, more reliable indicator to the attitude of these countries to foreign investors than the history of their response to foreigners and to Western influences during the era of the opening up of Asia between 1850 and 1900. The sections which follow give a country-by-country description of these Asian responses to foreigners.

CHINA

Our study must begin with China. Although the first European contacts with China had begun with the Portuguese as early as 1517 and trade had continued through Macau during the eighteenth century; although, too, the Russian penetration of Siberia had led to a succession of embassies in the late seventeenth and eighteenth centuries; it was finally the British East India Company, with its trading post at Canton, which provoked the opening up of China to global commerce. The first Anglo-Chinese War, 1839–42, known as the Opium War, was the catalyst for this momentous change. A war that was precipitated by the Qing government's justifiable efforts to suppress the pernicious, contraband trade in opium, was won by the superior fire power of British warships and followed by the 'unequal treaties' that gave Westerners special privileges in China including the granting in perpetuity of Hong Kong island to the British.

With the benefit of hindsight, conflict was probably inevitable, given on the one hand the outdated Chinese view of the outside world as a series of small nations bearing tribute to the Middle Kingdom and, on the other hand, Europe, led by England in the midst of its industrial revolution, with a strong military and naval power pushing aggressively to pursue business opportunities in the East. The large discrepancy in power relations led to a great change in China's relations with the outside world. Not only China's relative military weakness but also the West's ideas of scientific learning, individual freedom and economic growth all helped to make such a change inevitable.

In demanding diplomatic equality and commercial opportunity, Britain represented all the other Western powers. The Treaty of Nanking of 1842 abolished the Chinese monopoly of foreign trade at Canton, ceded Hong Kong to Britain and opened five ports to British residents and trade – Canton, Amoy, Foochow, Ningpo and Shanghai. It was the first of a number of further 'treaties' signed in the following decade with the French, the Americans and other Western powers. Under the terms of the treaty the British were granted rights of residence in the treaty ports and extraterritoriality (protection from Chinese laws). China ceded these privileges to Westerners under duress. A similar experience occurred when Commodore Perry arrived in Japan in 1853–4 but with very different results (see page 30).

The attitude of the Chinese authorities to foreign merchants and missionaries did not really undergo any change in the next fifty years, as the Anglo-French war with China in 1858–60 (the Second Opium War) and the Boxer Rebellion of 1898–1900 were to prove. It was only after the Anglo-French capture of Tientsin and Peking in 1860 that the Chinese government finally accepted the posting of Western ambassadors to the Imperial city, again under threat of force. The suppression of the Taiping Rebellion in 1864 was achieved with Western help, led by General Gordon. The Manchu Dynasty was thus given a new lease of life as China opened up for international trade and international diplomatic relations. The creation of the Chinese Imperial Maritime Customs Service under the leadership of Sir Robert Hart was the prime example of the acceptance by the Chinese authorities of the need for Western experts. The modernization drive of the late nineteenth century continued under the slogan: 'Chinese learning for fundamentals, Western learning for practical needs.'

Only after the founding of the Chinese Republic in 1911 (and then only in the late 1920s and early 1930s) for a brief period could China's potential for building a modern financial economy be observed. In the late 1980s and early 1990s this potential may be beginning to be finally realized as bond markets and stockmarkets are established in the PRC, and China's vast pool of domestic savings begins to be channelled towards the country's industrialization needs.

JAPAN

Japan's response to the West was very different from that of China. No wars were fought, no smuggling trade developed and no territory was lost. There was certainly a decade of domestic power struggle but out of it soon emerged a radical, new political system under which Japan moved rapidly to become a modern power by 1900.

Why did Japan react so differently from China? The Japanese had very different attitudes towards the outside world. The Chinese, long accustomed to the idea that the Middle Kingdom was the unique land of civilization, did not believe that there was much of value to be learnt from 'barbarians' and could not understand that this was a serious challenge to their national security. The Japanese, on the other hand, with their own sense of separate identity and their acute awareness of China, could understand the European system of equal and independent states. Well aware of all they had learnt over the ages from China, and even from Korea and India, they could readily see that there was much of great importance to be learnt from the West. Too accustomed to thinking of China as far larger, much older and more advanced than Japan, they had no supreme sense of cultural superiority, but rather a fear of inferiority. Thus, when menaced by the West, they did not look with disdain but rather with that combination of fear, resentment and narrow pride that one associates with nationalism.

Japan, too, was a much smaller country in which a new Western idea could spread and develop very quickly. As one old Chinese scholar has expressed it, 'Japan was like a glass of water in which a drop of ink would immediately discolour the whole. China was a vast pool . . .' in which ideas would spread very slowly, if at all (Prof. Hwang Yueh Chin).

Commodore Perry's arrival in July 1853 was at first strongly resisted. Even after the demonstration of US naval power had forced the signing of the Treaty of Kanagawa in 1854 and led to the opening of two small ports to American ships, the *samurai* lords or *daimyo*, especially in the south of Japan (Satsuma in southern Kuyshu and Choshu at the western tip of Honshu, in particular) continued to resist Western influence strongly for the next twenty years. The Government slogans of 'honour the Emperor' and 'expel the barbarian' were the rallying cries. A civil war between the old *shogunate* in Kyoto and the provincial *daimyo*, mainly in Choshu and Satsuma, resulted in the 1860s in the final collapse of the Tokugowa *shogunate* in 1868. In the meantime, the Satsuma samurai in Kagoshima had learnt the lesson about the inadequacy of traditional Japanese military power when the English navy bombarded the city in August 1863 in retaliation for the assassination of an English trader in the province. Satsuma made an indemnity payment of £25,000 but also developed a respect for and interest in the British navy. It immediately set about procuring Western ships with British aid, thus laying the foundation for what was to grow into the Imperial Japanese Navy.

Such flexibility and willingness to learn new ideas was also at the root of the amazing saga of the Meiji Restoration. No non-Western country has ever effected such a complete and mainly peaceful political revolution in such a short time so successfully as Japan between 1868 and 1900. It was effected by a small group of young men of *samurai* origin, who, having removed the *shogun*, restored the Meiji emperor to power. Appearance and reality, however, were quite different. The Meiji emperor was a mere figurehead.

The power rested with the oligarchs such as Kido, Okubo, Saigo and Ito Hirobumi (1841 to 1909) who effectively ruled Japan for the first forty years of the modern era. They were determined to modernize Japan and to make it a power equal to the West. Knowledge was to be sought throughout the world so as to strengthen the foundations of Imperial rule. Japan was to be modernized and strengthened through the use of Western knowledge because the only defence against the West lay in the creation of a rich country and a strong military adapting Western technology.

In this spirit, the reforming group of Meiji oligarchs proceeded to borrow the best from other Western countries – from Britain the navy and the railway system, from France the military, from Prussia the educational system, from the United States a system of national banking, and so on. Probably the most revolutionary step was the conscription law of 1873 making all men, regardless of social background, liable for three years of active military service. In addition, universal education and literacy was steadily established. The finances of the new regime were put in order within fifteen years with very little dependence on foreign borrowing. Land reform was carried out and the old feudal system effectively abolished. A new political constitution was put in place by 1880, based on the most up-to-date European models, with an upper house of peers, a national assembly, or diet, with 300 elected representatives and a ministerial system of government, under a prime minister and cabinet all answerable in theory to the supreme authority of the emperor. Despite the initial teething problems with this radical democratic reform, Japan had succeeded by the early twentieth century in its aim of creating a modern state and a military power which demonstrated its effectiveness in both the Sino-Japanese War of 1894–5 and, even more strikingly, in its defeat of Imperial Russia in the war of 1904–5. Meanwhile, the economic modernization of Japan had proceeded rapidly. Many Western analysts today seeking to understand the secrets of the Japanese economic miracle since 1945 may well find the foundations of this success in the Meiji period.

The whole foundation for Japan's modern industrial development was formed during the last thirty years of the nineteenth century. In fact, the financial problems of the new Meiji government resulted in a policy of economic retrenchment by which, in November 1880, the government sold all non-strategic government industries, such as shipbuilding, armaments, textiles, steel and transport. Most were sold at very low prices to leading businesspeople or even government officials and for ten years did not show any great profitability. Nevertheless, this initial step contributed to the eventual concentration of much of Japanese industry in the hands of a few giant companies, the *zaibatsu*. They were only, with rare exceptions, the old trading houses such as Mitsui and Sumitomo. More often they were successful *samurai* entrepreneurs such as Iwasaki Yataro, who founded Mitsubishi and developed the first major shipping line. Another example was

Shibusawa Etichi who founded the Osaka spinning mill and was the father of Japan's modern textile industry.

By the 1890s Japanese exports had commenced, led by the cotton spinning industry which employed about 63 per cent of all factory workers at that time. Simultaneously, the Nippon Yusen Kaisha (NYK) Shipping Line was founded under Mitsubishi leadership in 1885. An early pattern was established of government and industry co-operating in leading strategic industries and also of vertical integration, for example, from the cotton spinning factory to the international shipping line which was in time to make Japan's export machine – known as 'Japan Inc.' – a fearsomely efficient competitor in the twentieth-century world.

From the beginning, however, Japan's economic growth depended on exports. Foreign trade was necessary as a source of raw materials, especially minerals and fuels and also of machinery imports. However, the percentage of foreign trade accounted for in Japan's economy as a whole remained low and, relative to European countries, remains low to this day. Japan's large population of 120 million and its enormous domestic consumption is still a key to the growth of its economy. It should never be forgotten that Japan was isolated from the entire world for over two hundred years from 1640 to 1853. During that period its economy, its culture and its internal transport system all developed rapidly without any foreign help. Many of the characteristics of modern Japan were set during the Tokogowa period. However, it is the remarkable story of the forty years from 1870 to 1910 during which the Meiji oligarchs led Japan into the modern world, politically and economically, which really gives the best understanding of how Japan is ruled politically and how Japan handles the Western challenge today as it did a century ago.

There is still today, as in the 1880s, a tremendous appetite for Western novelties, fashions and new products. But it is also true to say that in most leading product markets, the market share (including Western banks'), rarely exceeds 2 or 3 per cent. Such is the stranglehold of the large domestic corporations, the *zaibatsu* or, as they have been known since 1945, the *keiretsu*, that it is rare for a Western company, even IBM, to gain a leading market share.

JAPAN'S ECONOMY 1900–40

There was a boom in the Japanese economy in the early part of this century which depended very little on foreign investment. The population grew from 43 million in 1900 to 73 million in 1940. Domestic consumption was important but there was also export demand for cottons and bicycles and other light industrial products. Government expenditure increased rapidly in the military sphere creating a domestic market for Japan's heavy industries before these could be sold in the West. The First World War in Europe also increased demand for Japanese manufactured goods which, for the first time, expanded into other Asian countries. By 1920 Japan had become a creditor nation with gold resources of more than Y2 billion – a six-fold increase in six years. This was followed by high inflation and a credit collapse during the 1920s. It is very interesting to note that the great Kanto earthquake of 1923 did not adversely affect Japan's economy. In fact it set off a construction boom and this might be the pattern of any future such event in Japan, despite the large property losses which could result.

During the 1920s and 1930s a key indicator in tracking the health of Japan's economy is to look at the price of rice and the price of silk which were the major basic products of Japanese agriculture and also major exports. Even today rice is not merely symbolic but essential to land values and to political life in Japan. The recent decision by the Liberal-Democrat Party (LDP) government to let the domestic price of rice fall gradually over a period of years to the world price will have profound effects on Japan domestically. It was the perceived vulnerability of Japan's economy to this basic shortage of raw materials, oil, food and other commodities, which led directly to the decision to expand into China and after 1941 to the Pacific War. Major targets of Japan's thrust south were the oilfields of Indonesia. Today there is close economic co-operation between Japan and Indonesia effectively guaranteeing Japanese industry a steady, cheap supply of liquid natural gas (LNG).

The zaibatsu system was the key to Japan's economic development both before and (in a less visible form) after the war. During the 1920s and 1930s Mitsui and Mitsubishi were probably the two largest private economic empires in the world, each having more than one hundred companies within their conglomerates and employing about 1 million people in Japan and outside. They were involved in mining, manufacturing, trading, shipping and banking. At the centre each was tightly controlled by a single family. But the policy of these giant combines was also closely intertwined with Japan's national policy and strategic interests. The capital investment which they were able to make in new technologies derived from their enormous size and financial strength. In 1945 the Americans saw the destruction of these military industrial complexes as one of their main aims. However, these giant combines had positive effects too and the strength of the Japanese economy today still owes a great deal to the core strength of these *keiretsu* groups. However, in Japan today, as in 1930, more than half of the manufacturing labour force is employed in small businesses. Unlike the Chinese, the core unit of Japanese society tends to be not the family but the company, whether large or small, encompassing all aspects of life, somewhat like the old *samurai* military units.

Japan, like Siam, was able to absorb Western ideas without losing its own unique culture. The achievement was the more remarkable when it is seen how rapidly it was affected on other levels during the Meiji period. In particular, the creation of a modern political democracy is striking. By 1925 Japan had achieved universal male suffrage and the electorate had increased from 400,000 in 1890 to 12 million (out of a total population of 63 million).

Among the most perceptive writers about Japan was the American historian Ruth Benedict whose book *The Chrysanthemum and the Sword* reflects the two sides of the Japanese character, the aesthetic and the militaristic. She wrote the book to try to prepare American officers for their occupation of Japan after 1945 (Benedict, 1946). Despite the pacifism which has characterized the country and the constitution since 1945 few Western observers doubt that the military side of the Japanese character still exists although it is not dominant today. Unlike Germany at the end of the Nazi period, the Japanese have rarely exhibited a sense of guilt. There are still political arguments about the re-writing of history textbooks used in Japanese schools to reflect the establishment view that Japan's advance into Manchuria in 1931 was justifiable and that atrocities in China and Korea were never actually committed. All these historical factors are still relevant when we consider relations between Japan and its Asian neighbours – not only China, Korea and Taiwan, former areas of Japanese colonization – but also the Philippines, Singapore, Malaysia and Thailand, which were all occupied by Japanese forces between 1942 and 1945. It is true to say that the 'Greater East Asia Co-prosperity Sphere' which Japan professed to be establishing during its drive for empire in the early 1940s has been recreated albeit in a purely economic rather than military sense and that there is, therefore, a great deal of ambivalence on the part of those receiving Japanese investment, technology and trade today in these areas of Asia (see Figure 3.1).

Japan's response to the West, therefore, also took the form of imitating Western imperialism and forming a colonial empire as Britain, France, Holland and even the United States had all done in other parts of Asia. In turn the response of the conquered Asian nations to the Japanese took the form of nationalism, particularly in the Philippines, Indonesia and Vietnam.

THE US IMPRINT ON ASIA SINCE 1945

Before 1850 East Asia was isolated. Its people were rigidly controlled under autocratic rule and generally not permitted to travel overseas, to trade, to vote or to have any kind of personal freedom, unlike their contemporaries in the Western world. Despite the ensuing century of Western contacts in Asia, it was only after 1945 and thanks to the Americans that Asians in general began to enjoy the benefits of free trade, freedom of movement, free press and freedom of religion. This is particularly true of Japan after 1945, and is also true of Taiwan and Korea – all three were occupied by US forces and deeply influenced by US culture. The American influence is less obviously present in the Chinese city states of Hong Kong and Singapore which have had a British

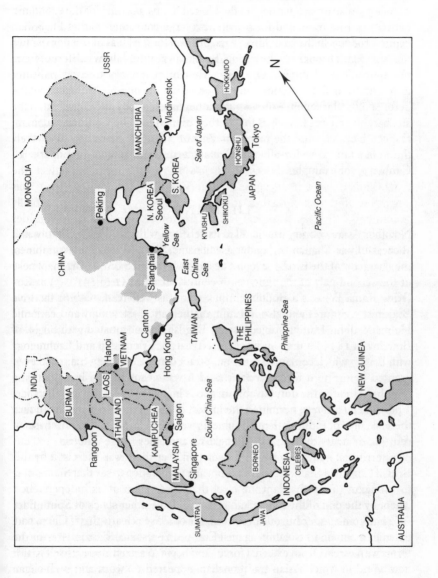

Figure 3.1. The Greater East Asia Co-prosperity Sphere

tradition. However, most of the privileged Chinese in these cities today are educated in American universities.

Asia owes an enormous debt to the United States, not only for the economic benefits of free trade and for providing a large consumer market for Asia's export products in the past thirty years, but also for the ideas of freedom which the Americans brought to the region. But Asian reality is always different from the appearance of things. The Asian view of democracy today is radically different from the American idea. For Asians, economic freedom comes before political freedom – they would rather have stability and consensus than an anarchic free press such as that of the Philippines. The Confucian ideas of respect, hierarchy and the moral integrity of rulers are more important than the democratic free-for-all which characterizes parliaments in London or Canberra, for example.

THAILAND

No other Asian country has handled its relations with the West so simply and successfully as Thailand or, under its old name, Siam. Much of this was due to the character of the two benevolent despots who ruled Siam during the whole of the second part of the nineteenth century, from 1851 to 1910. Mongkut (King Rama IV) was a Buddhist monk who was well-read, both in the Pali Buddhist scriptures and also in Latin, mathematics, astronomy and English. He made all his leading subjects study English. He negotiated with Sir John Bowring in 1855 (entirely in English) a Treaty of Friendship and Commerce with Britain which contained more important concessions than Siam had ever granted before to a foreign power (and it was negotiated in less than one month). It limited the duty payable on goods imported by British merchants to 3 per cent *ad valorem*, permitted the import of opium duty free and laid down the scale of export duties. British subjects were to be permitted to purchase or rent land near the capital, Bangkok, and they were subject to the extraterritorial system by which jurisdiction over them was exercised by the British Consul in Siam. It is perhaps not an exaggeration to say that Siam owed to Mongkut (more than anyone else) the preservation of its independence when, by the end of the nineteenth century, all the other states of South East Asia had come under European control. He could see clearly that if China had failed to maintain its isolation against European pressure, Siam must come to terms with threats from external forces and begin to accommodate itself to the new world in which Asian traditionalism appeared outworn and inefficient. Thus, he not only opened up Siam's trade with the outside world, he welcomed foreign residents and gave them extensive privileges. He brought in many Western advisers and was intensely interested in science and education. He promoted the building of canals, the construction of roads, shipbuilding, the teaching of foreign languages and he established a new coinage.

Mongkut's work was taken over by his son Chulalongkorn (King Rama V) who had been educated as a boy by Mrs. Leonowens, the famous governess of *The King and I*. Chulalongkorn took his father's reforms one step further and established two English schools in Bangkok to which the aristocracy were forced to send their children. He abolished slavery and reformed the military system and taxation. The long-term results of these measures have been most striking, especially by contrast with Siam's two neighbours, French Indochina (now Vietnam) and Burma, ruled by the British. Siam's peasantry became a strong and independent class, free from the ancient serfdom, owning its own land, depositing money in the savings bank, in fact acquiring a stake in the country. This is still true today and it is a striking feature of the Thai character that the people are free, in the various senses of the word, and independent capitalists. Chulalongkorn also encouraged the building of railways. He was able to fend off French encroachments on the border of Laos by playing off the British and the French against each other and becoming a buffer state between the two.

In all these fields – education, transport, finance, diplomacy – these two remarkable Kings of Siam depended on European advisers. At the same time, just as in Thailand today, they used foreigners to modernize successfully without losing any of their traditional culture and confidence. Thailand today is one of the most open countries for foreign investors, up to a point. The foreigner is encouraged to come and place his or her capital in Thailand in the freest possible way, as long as it is in the interests of Thailand. The long-term planning that has characterized the Thai civil service for decades was begun in the late nineteenth century under the reigns of Mongkut and Chulalongkorn. The monarchy has, in fact, been one of the key elements in Siam's, and now Thailand's, stability, confidence and successful response to the Western challenge.

KOREA

Before 1880 Korea was probably the most isolated country in the world with virtually no external trade or outside contacts. Once a year a tributary mission was sent to Peking but the Qing Dynasty exercised little if no control, except in name, over the Korean peninsula. Korea was a small kingdom by Chinese, if not by European, standards. (The total population of the Korean peninsula today is just over 60 million making it slightly larger than England or France.) Korea's geographic problem is that it is at the point where three great empires – China, Japan and the Soviet Union – meet and conflict. This strategic location has meant that more often than not the peninsula has been divided over the course of the centuries. The present division between North and South Korea is more complete and tragic in its human consequences. In medieval times Korea was divided into the states of Koguryo, Paekche and

Silla which each exercised a dominant power at different times, with Japanese or Chinese influence playing a role. Even today there are many political differences within South Korea.

The last years of the Yi Dynasty (1392 to 1910) were characterized by the abrupt entry of foreign influences. The Japanese, playing the same role as the Americans in Japan in the 1850s, forced the opening of Korea in 1876. American influence was also present through the strong missionary effort. There was a brief decade of Chinese ascendancy from 1882 to 1894 but, after the victory of Japan in the Sino-Japanese War, the Japanese became the dominant power in Korea. The Russians meanwhile continued to expand into the Far East with the building of the Trans-Siberian Railway in the 1890s, but their defeat by Japan in 1905 left Japan in a strong position, ruling Taiwan, dominating Korea and expanding in Manchuria. Despite the growth of a strong nationalist spirit in Korea, Japan annexed the country in August 1910 and Korea became a full Japanese colony. Although Japanese colonial rule lasted only for thirty-five years, or the span of a single generation, it had a profound and negative impact on the Korean economy and culture, suppressing nationalism and imposing the Japanese language and administration.

Korea, then, had the double misfortune of being geographically placed in the strategic 'cockpit' of North East Asia between three great powers, and also, deeply influenced as it was by the Confucian culture of China and isolated from the outside world, being perhaps the least well-prepared of the Asian nations to meet the Western challenge. During the last fifty years the country has suffered the set back of becoming a Japanese colony, the devastation of the 1950–3 war, and the rule of the northern half of the peninsula by the most absolute communist dictatorship. In this perspective the economic renaissance of South Korea since 1960 is all the more amazing. South Korea's finest hour was the staging of the 1988 Olympics in Seoul, which brought it full international recognition of the country's achievements. Nevertheless, a lingering suspicion of foreigners remains from the centuries-old tradition of the 'hermit kingdom'.

South Korea remains a difficult country in which to do business and in which to invest. Nevertheless, the high proportion of the population (around 25 per cent) who are Christian, and the country's strong links with the United States, do much to mitigate these characteristics. Korea in the 1990s is facing a situation somewhat parallel to the 1890s with the rising economic and financial power of Japan, China in transition and the Soviet Union possibly losing its status as a superpower, with incalculable consequences for the political future of North Korea. There is a fascinating trend, apparent since 1988, whereby Japan has been cultivating closer relations with North Korea, on the one hand; while China and the Soviet Union develop trade and other links with South Korea.

INDONESIA

In 1292 the Polos, on their way home from China, visited Sumatra stopping at the port of Perlak where they found that the numerous Muslim traders had converted the natives to Islam. This was the first and most lasting foreign influence on the Indonesian archipelago, where today 90 per cent of a population of nearly 200 million professes to be Muslim. The later arrival of the Portuguese (mainly in Timor) and then the Dutch had an important but less lasting influence. The Dutch ruled Indonesia from the time of the formation of the Dutch East India Company in 1602 until 1948. But it is surprising, considering this long period of colonial rule, how shallow the European influence has been on the culture. Economically, Indonesia has always been well endowed with natural resources, not only rich in its plantations but also, more recently, in the important discoveries of natural gas and oil. However, the need to provide for the large and dense population of Java has meant that per capita income remains low even in the midst of plenty. During the period of Dutch colonial rule much of the wealth of Indonesia was drained off finishing up in Amsterdam and the Hague. The fierce anti-colonial struggle of the aftermath of the Second World War left a bitter taste in Indonesia. It deprived the country of much needed foreign capital for several decades. In the 1980s the attitude of the Indonesian ruling elite began to change with the arrival of a new, post-colonial generation in power. Today there is a much more relaxed acceptance of the need for foreign capital, foreign technology and management in Indonesia.

MALAYSIA/SINGAPORE

Britain, or at least the East India Company, acquired Penang in 1786 for purely naval purposes. The architect of the future states of Singapore was Sir Stamford Raffles, who had been a successful Lieutenant Governor of Java from 1811 to 1816 (during the Anglo-Dutch alliance following the Napoleonic War) where, among other things, he abolished slavery. His dream of making Batavia (now called Jakarta) the centre of a new British Empire in the Indonesian islands failed, but on 28 January 1819 he founded the port of Singapore which was to become the strategic port commanding the Malacca Straits, still today the funnel for the oil tanker trade from the Gulf to East Asia. The Straits Settlements developed gradually during the nineteenth century, with the British generally leaving the local sultans in power while controlling overseas trade and maintaining naval supremacy.

As with the Dutch, the British influence in the Malay peninsula and in the British ruled territories of Sarawak, and North Borneo (the eastern portion of modern Malaysia) was neither very deep nor lasting. In all these scattered regions the British acquired an empire, in Sir John Seeley's apt phrase 'in a fit of absence of mind', and without any coherent purpose except for expanding trade and commerce (Sir John Seeley, *The Expansion of England*). The original attraction of the East Indies had been that of the spice islands. The subsequent development of rubber plantations greatly accelerated the economic development of Malaya. The British North Borneo Company concentrated mainly on timber concessions of teak and mahogany. But the difficulties of communication, transport and climate mitigated against any large or lasting European settlements.

THE PHILIPPINES

The Philippines is often regarded as a country with more affinity culturally and politically with Latin America than with Asia because of its Roman Catholic and Spanish characteristics. In fact, the underlying language and culture of the Philippines is not very different from the Bahasa Malay of Malaysia and the Indonesian islands. The Spanish influence on the Philippines began in the early 1500s and, with the annual visit of the Manila galleon bringing silver from Mexico, continued until 1898 when the American Commodore Dewey sunk the Spanish fleet in Manila Bay and the Philippines became the first American colony in Asia. Following the Proclamation of Filipino Independence by Emilio Aguinaldo, US foreign policy was somewhat divided and, while the Filipinos wanted independence, the Americans provided a colonial administration of a very different type from the European powers with a Washington appointed Governor-General but a popularly elected Senate and Legislature in Manila. The United States had thus, by the 1930s and within a short period of time, introduced an advanced form of political democracy into the Philippines.

The impact of American political institutions was, however, as elsewhere in Asia, a fairly superficial one. The greatest and most beneficial impact of the American influence was the spread of education, as the spread of the Roman Catholic religion had been the greatest legacy of the Spanish. The economy, meanwhile, was tied to that of the United States and dependent on American largesse. This dependency has been a continuing characteristic, along with the presence of the American military bases which provide much employment and foreign currency. The Japanese occupation of the Philippines between 1941 and 1944 left some bitterness but also accelerated, as it did elsewhere in South East Asia, the coming of independence in 1947. However, many economic problems remained and the Americans continued to dominate Filipino trade and investment. Political corruption has been a constant theme in the Philippine governments both before and since independence, culminating in the rule of Marcos.

4

RISK AND REWARD ANALYSIS OF ASIAN COUNTRIES TODAY

INTRODUCTION

Sir John Templeton (founder of Templeton College, Oxford) says in his investment principles that 'social and political awareness' are among the key attributes of a successful investment manager, meaning that it is important to be aware of risks inherent in an unstable or inequitable political situation in a country, of pollution and environmental risks for any company, of labour unions, and of social and political strife that may result.

This can be taken a step further by saying that ideally an investment manager should have an historical awareness: that is, of the character of a people and a nation as revealed in their actions and reactions in past centuries. A national character does not change: a people's strengths and weaknesses tend to be enduring. Risk and reward, then, for the present day investor in Asia may depend on an analysis of past events in China, Japan and other Asian countries, on the response to foreign traders and investors in the nineteenth century, and on the forms which that response took.

For instance, currency stability depends a great deal on the popular 'folk' memory of past inflation. China shares the experience of hyperinflation in the Shanghai of 1948, with Germany which also saw worthless paper currency in wheelbarrow loads in the 1923 Weimar Republic. As a consequence, both the German and Chinese peoples have a deep and abiding fear of inflation and the political and economic chaos which follows in its wake.

It is not a luxury for an investment manager to study the history of the countries in which he or she invests. It is a vital and inherent part of the analytical task of assessing risk and assessing performance potential.

Risk analysis is technically an activity undertaken by those who lend money, such as bankers or insurance analysts who are trying to protect assets, rather than those who invest their capital for long-term gains, that is, fund managers. Therefore, although the succeeding chapter will draw greatly on the work of commercial bankers working in Asia and analyzing the risks affecting each individual country, I will attempt to go one step further and assess not only the risk for an investor (as opposed to a banker), but also to evaluate the potential rewards in terms of portfolio performance or the growth or recovery of share prices in that particular country. The two approaches are inherently different.

It is frequently the case where, at one and the same time, the banker sees a country as being a particularly bad credit risk, and an investment manager may perceive it as a very attractive investment opportunity. This is because the majority of analysts have focused on the downside risks which are, therefore, fully discounted, rather than the upside opportunities which are not.

A classic example of this was South Korea in 1984, which had the highest sovereign debt at the time of any Asian country. All of its debt service ratios and other key indicators were very negative. Most bankers that one consulted at the time were extremely unwilling to make fresh loans to South Korea. Political stability had remained questionable ever since the assassination of President Park in 1979. The rise in oil prices and the world recession in 1981 had hit South Korea badly. There were domestic political tensions and strong pressures from the unions. Inflation had averaged 20 per cent during the previous five years. And yet, South Korea came out of this crisis in the early 1980s with a renewed vigour which only those who had studied the history and character of the Korean people could have foreseen. The strong work ethic which had enabled the Koreans to build up their industries, such as steel, shipbuilding, cars and the massive construction industry which had undertaken vast projects in the Middle East during the previous decade, all testified to the almost military discipline and commitment to work, to savings and to nation building which characterized the Koreans more than any other Asian nationality. On average the Koreans worked almost fifty hours a week, harder than any other people in the world. Meanwhile, the tiny Seoul stockmarket was capitalized at $3 billion compared to the nation's GNP of $75 billion. A percipient observer might well have compared this situation with that of Japan twenty years earlier.

The foundations were in place for a tremendous growth in the capital market, which would reflect and follow the remarkable economic growth which had already been achieved. The leading *chaebol* – Daewoo, Hyundai, Samsung, Goldstar and others – represented a strong foundation for the internationalization of the Korean business sector in the same way as the Japanese *zaibatsu* had spearheaded Japan's overseas export drive in earlier decades. So, despite the obvious risks, Korea proved to be an outstanding investment opportunity in 1984. In fact, the stockmarket capitalization grew by twenty-five times between 1984 and 1990. The number of domestic investors in Korea also grew by almost thirty times. Real estate prices in Seoul soared. Any foreign investor who had taken a gamble on the Korean market at that point would have seen his or her investment multiply by more than ten times in any of the leading Korean country funds, the first of which, the Korea Fund Inc., was listed on the New York Stock Exchange late in 1984.

Even the national currency, the won, appreciated against the dollar as Korea succeeded in turning from deficit into a handsome surplus and paid back a large part of its foreign debt in the process.

Another example was Indonesia in 1987–8. Although the history of Indonesia in the colonial period does not give grounds for optimism to the dispassionate historian and analyst, nevertheless Indonesia, like Korea, had escaped from its colonial masters and was determined to establish a strong national identity, to grow rapidly and to provide jobs for its vast population, especially in Java. Under President Suharto, there had been a new trend towards stability – a political and economic philosophy had been formulated for the nation and the key to the successful implementation of this was a small band of highly educated technocrats (often called the Berkeley Mafia) who had masterminded Indonesia's economic planning during the previous twenty years. The recent and most difficult challenge with which they dealt was the collapse of world oil prices in the spring of 1986. Up to then oil had represented more than 80 per cent, sometimes 90 per cent, of Indonesia's total exports.

So, once again, a banker looking at the credit risk of Indonesia in 1987 would have been deeply pessimistic about its chances of being able to repay loans when its principal export commodity had halved in price. However, looking beneath the surface and talking to the highly intelligent group of people in the Ministry of Finance and the Ministry of Industry in Jakarta, it was apparent that a major shift was taking place in Indonesia's composition of exports, towards drawing on the low wage manufacturing base and also the rapid growth in wood products and minerals, especially gold. By the end of the 1980s oil represented only 40 per cent of Indonesia's exports and the growth in the non-oil sector proved to be remarkable. Simultaneously, the Ministry of Finance and its capital markets agency, Bapepam, had taken a decision to free up the rigid controls on the financial and banking sector and to try to encourage the growth of a capital market in Jakarta for the first time since the Dutch colonial period. The sleepy Indonesian stockmarket consisted of only twenty-four listings, of which only eight were available to foreign investors. Few fund managers bothered to visit Jakarta since the volume of turnover was practically negligible so, not only was there very little to buy, but it did not have much prospect of appreciation.

Here, the key to the investment opportunity was in understanding the shift in political sentiment at the top level of the government and among the technocrats. The willingness to encourage foreign capital and, in particular, foreign portfolio investments led directly to the boom in the Indonesian capital market in 1989–90. The successful reorientation of Indonesia away from its sole dependence on oil was a unique example among the members of OPEC who viewed oil as a God-given boon which would always be there to pay for any grandiose projects. The Indonesians, however, were more pragmatic and flexible and perceived the need to diversify and also to provide employment for a population which would surpass 200 million before the year 2000. Once again, the risk and reward analysis was a complex task, taking in a set of very different cultural, economic and political factors and essentially having faith in the ability of the technocrats to succeed in their bold policies.

HOW TO MEASURE RISK

Risk measurement is certainly an art rather than a science. This is why the historical perspective helps a great deal in being able to assess the probabilities of political crisis and instability or expropriation of foreign investors' assets. There cannot, in fact, be a precisely mathematical model to account for all the different factors which come to play in the risk analysis of any given country. Nevertheless, one can attempt to separate out these different factors and to grade them according to the track record of a nation.

First there is natural risk, which includes earthquake, typhoon, hurricane, floods, drought, famine, failure of monsoon, epidemics, etc. Second, there is political risk which, in the first category, includes revolution, *coup d'état*, invasion, civil war, and in the second category there is the milder form of political risk represented by a change of government, either of a prime minister, of a political party, or even a key cabinet official who may change the economic policy of a nation as it affects foreign investors. For instance, tax rates may be appreciably increased or the ability to remit profits out of the country may be restricted. Thirdly, there is economic risk which includes recession, a slowdown, currency devaluation, commodity price changes, inflation, foreign debt, protectionism, repudiation or expropriation of foreign assets. Fourthly, there is the market risk specific to each national stockmarket, which depends essentially on the price level of the market represented by the price earnings ratio, which may also include the inherent volatility of the national index or leading shares and the volume of turnover which represents investors' ability to sell.

REWARD ANALYSIS

The first and most tangible method of measuring rewards or national performance is, of course, in the GNP growth rate over a period of years, and the annual total returns in US dollars of the capital markets. Then taking a deeper look the annual corporate earnings growth of the leading listed companies should be measured over a period of twenty years and the performance of the local currency against the US dollar over a long period should be included in the evaluation. Allied to this is the inflation rate which may be used as a barometer, a national thermometer of price fever.

In trying to build the foundations of future predictions, these will, as always, be based on past performance. One key to this analysis in Asia is to measure the national savings rate as a percentage of income, since it so convincingly displays the Confucian work ethic and the urge to save for future educational and family needs. Later in my analysis there will be many other more intangible factors which may be included in the forecast, such as the impact of new products and technologies, and the globalization of the Asian economic miracle which has carried many people from East Asia to California and opened up new trading links and new markets for Asian exports and capital flows. The acceleration of this two-way flow is indeed one of the strongest arguments for the continued growth of Asia in the next twenty years.

ECONOMIC RISK ANALYSIS IN HISTORY

Risk is a very ancient concept but risk management is relatively modern. Even by studying only the last two centuries since the French Revolution of 1789, it is possible to put in perspective the main movements of modern history as they have affected investors. The main risks may be summarized as follows:

1. Revolution and expropriation of foreign assets.
2. Civil war or disorder.
3. Nationalization of assets.
4. Inflation and the collapse of monetary values.

The French Revolution was really the first modern example of wholesale confiscation of property belonging to the aristocracy and to foreigners by a new and radical regime. In fact, in many parts of Europe in the nineteenth century and in Tsarist Russia there were few legal protections against arbitrary confiscation of property by the ruling power. Only in eighteenth-century England did the legal and parliamentary system and the rule of habeas corpus fully protect individuals and their property. Other examples in the nineteenth century may include the revolutions of 1848 in central Europe.

The first instance of a communist revolution was in Russia in 1917, which resulted in a large loss of wealth for foreign investors including many French bond holders who had invested in Russian railways, many British capitalists who had built factories and made loans in pre-revolutionary Russia and, of course, the capitalist class of Russians themselves. The event, when it happened, was almost wholly unexpected except by a few perceptive observers who had followed the gradual collapse of order during the Tsarist regime and the following brief period of rule by Kerensky. Capitalists are often myopic and fail to see the social ferment building up. Incredible as it seems, it is reported that the St. Petersburg stock exchange hit its all time high just before Lenin arrived at the Finland station in November 1917. The post-war Weimahr Republic in Germany in 1923 represents the *locus classicus* of hyperinflation, wiping out many large and small investors. It was again preceded by a stockmarket boom in Berlin when (as in Latin America today) local share values expressed in the fast depreciating marks actually did, for certain periods, show a good gain measured in foreign currencies. However, very few investors were able to sell out at the right time, faced with a situation where people were carrying their money to buy groceries in wheelbarrows.

The same situation occurred again in Shanghai in 1948 when prices rose seventy times within a year. The wealth of many middle class Chinese was wiped out by this phenomenon before the communists took power in 1949. Once again, as in 1917 Russia, there was confusion and there was still optimism among many people who thought they would be able to save their property and savings. Indeed, it took two or three years before foreign investors and local factory owners were fully nationalized and expropriated. One notable example was Jardine Matheson, the leading British trading house in the Far East, which had large property holdings in Shanghai in 1950. The corporate and family memory of the Keswicks has been deeply marked by this bitter experience in the early years of communist China. Jardine's early move to change its legal domicile from Hong Kong to Bermuda in 1984 at the very start of the Sino-British talks on the future of Hong Kong, was surely based on this deep and abiding suspicion of the Chinese communists which is common to all those who experienced the events of 1949–50. In this sense it is vital for the reader who wishes to assess the risk of Hong Kong in 1997 not only to study the history of 1949 China but also to be aware of the reactions of the principal companies and investors affected by that experience.

Another aspect of risk is to be able to make a consistent measurement of investment value. In Asia in recent years there have been extraordinary booms and busts, particularly in the capital markets. Volatility is characteristic of a high growth region with a rapid circulation of new-found wealth. Japan has been one classic example with the stockmarket boom being built up over a number of decades but reaching its climax in the late 1980s, with high price earnings multiples and absurd valuations of companies when compared to their underlying assets or sales volume. Even more extraordinary was the case of the Taiwan stockmarket which rose by ten times in three years up to 1989 and then collapsed to about 15 per cent of its previous value. These Asian examples are reminiscent of the South Sea Bubble of 1720 and many other cases of money madness which have been chronicled by Charles Mackay in his classic nineteenth-century work, *Extraordinary Popular Delusions and the Madness of Crowds*. Mackay comments, 'Men, it has been well said, think in herds: it will be seen that they go mad in herds, while they only recover their senses slowly, and one by one' (Mackay, 1841). So, even while maintaining an optimistic view of the Asian economic outlook in the 1990s and the financial opportunities which it offers, it is well to keep in mind a view of the inherent values and not to lose sight of them. In China today, for instance, there are still occurring stockmarket booms in Shenzhen and Shanghai reminiscent of these earlier waves of money madness in Western and other Asian markets.

Risk, then, is not only the risk of being expropriated in a revolution but also of losing assets by being sucked into an over priced 'money mad' market.

Table 4.1. Comparative inflation rates of Asian countries, 1981–90

	Average CPI	Ranking[1]
Japan	2.1	1
Singapore	2.3	2
Taiwan	3.1	3
Malaysia	3.5	4
Thailand	4.5	5
Korea	6.5	6
China[2]	6.9	7
Hong Kong	8.2	8
Indonesia	8.7	9
Philippines	14.5	10

1. Markets are ranked in each category with a scale from 1 to 10. 1 being the best and 10 being the worst.
2. RPI figure, not CPI

INFLATION IN ASIA

Table 4.1 attempts to assess the longer-term inflation outlook in Asia by using the ten-year averages for each country during the 1980s. It is readily apparent that Japan and Singapore consistently score highest in terms of this criterion. In fact, this table may be the best guide to political and economic stability. Earlier in this chapter the inflation rate was described as a very sensitive barometer of national fever, reflecting economic stresses and consequent political strains. This is more than a theoretical economist's view. It is borne out by events in China in 1988–9 when inflation and the democracy movement rose and fell together. Nor is it accidental that the attempted military *coup d'états* in both Manila and Bangkok coincided with a rapid increase in consumer prices in both those fast developing cities. Indeed, the Philippines does appear, both qualitatively and quantitatively, to be different from all the other Asian countries in terms of risks judged on this criterion.

In compiling Table 4.2, which takes an overall view of Asian risk and reward ratios, the following factors have been taken into consideration:

1. Political risk has been calculated according to the individual country commentaries which follow in Chapter 5. Risks evaluated include change of government and policies but also the possiblity of military *coup d'états*, revolutions, invasions and expropriation of foreign assets.

Table 4.2. Asian risk and reward ratios

	Risk[1]			Reward[2]		
	Political	Inflation	Currency vs US $	Population	GNP	Capita market
Japan	1	1	2	8	5	5
Singapore	2	2	1	7	3	3
Thailand	3	5	1	2	1	5
Malaysia	3	4	2	1	2	3
Taiwan	5	3	2	6	2	7
S Korea	5	6	3	5	1	4
Hong Kong	7	8	1	5	3	6
China	8	8	5	3	2	–
Indonesia	6	9	4	2	4	8
Philippines	8	10	5	2	7	9

1. 1 = low risk, 10 = high risk
2. 1 = high potential, 10 = low potential

2. Economic risks have been largely concentrated on inflation rates and the possibility of currency devaluation.
3. Population growth can be looked at either as an economic problem and threat or as a marketing opportunity. For the purposes of this book demographic growth and personal income growth are multiplied in the overall equation to reach economic growth potential in each country.
4. GNP growth is based on the twenty-year averages which have been calculated and extrapolated forward into the 1990s.
5. For the capital market we have calculated performance, volatility, turnover and liquidity as well as price earnings ratios, dividend yields and interest rates.

All of these factors have been considered in giving a risk reward score to the stockmarket in each country.

Chapter 5 now goes on to give a country-by-country breakdown of whichever of the following are relevant – political and economic risk, inflation risk, exchange rate risk and foreign trade risk.

5

COUNTRY-BY-COUNTRY
RISK ANALYSIS

CHINA

Table 5.1 gives details of the overall economic performance of China from 1970 to 1990.

Table 5.1. Economic profile of China, 1970–90

	Exchange rate ag. US $	GNP/ GDP growth (%)	(Inflation) RPI	Trade surplus/ (deficit) (US $mn)	P/E	Total turnover (US $mn)	Market year-end closing	Market capital (US $bn)
1970		23.2						
1971		4.0						
1972	2.240 1	2.9						
1973	2.020 2	8.3						
1974	1.839 7	1.0						
1975	1.966 3	8.3						
1976	1.880 3	−3.0						
1977	1.730 0	7.8	2.49					
1978	1.5771	12.3	0.88					
1979	1.496 2	7.0	1.97					
1980	1.530 3	6.4	7.41	(1 800)				
1981	1.745 5	4.9	2.50	0				
1982	1.922 7	8.3	2.05	3 000				
1983	1.980 9	9.8	1.24	800				
1984	2.795 7	13.5	2.83	(1 300)				
1985	3.201 5	13.1	8.82	(14 900)				
1986	3.722 1	7.8	5.99	(12 000)				
1987	3.722 1	9.4	7.32	(3 800)				
1988	3.722 1	10.8	18.50	(7 700)				
1989	4.722 1	3.9	17.80	(6 700)				
1990	5.222 1	5.0	2.10	8 700	45.55	144.0	439.0	0.25

Note: Stockmarket data relates to Shanghai's Stock Exchange only.

Having taken a long view of Chinese history it becomes apparent that it is extremely difficult to predict anything about China's future political direction and, therefore, to measure in any sense the investment risk in the People's Republic of China today. Past convulsions and changes of dynasty have frequently occurred unexpectedly and suddenly. The attitude to foreigners has also undergone dramatic swings during the last 150 years, from the Opium War in the 1840s to the establishment of the Imperial Chinese Customs Service under Western expatriate management during the era of reform in 1860 to 1880, followed by the dramatic anti-foreign sentiment of the Boxer Rebellion and the siege of the Peking legations in 1900. The last years of the Manchu Dynasty and the republican era of 1911–49 again saw a period of openness and Westernization but the arrival of Mao Zi Dong and the communists in power in October 1949 heralded thirty years of Chinese isolation and self-sufficiency; a return, in fact, to the Middle Kingdom mentality of earlier centuries which reached its apogee during the Cultural Revolution and once again the attacks on Western embassies in Peking in 1967.

While the 1980s have seen a remarkable opening up of the Chinese economy and of China as a whole to Westerners, both as tourists and businesspeople, anyone with an historical perspective will realize that there must be a probability that the pendulum will, in due course, swing back and that China will once again stress its self-reliance. At the present time, the direction of policy in Peking seems firmly set against political reform on the one hand, but towards increasing economic reform on the other hand. The economic experiment of the 1980s has had mixed reviews and since 1989 there has been a distinct slowdown. Nevertheless, the Coastal Area Development Programme proposed by Zhao Ziyang in 1988 was a remarkable echo of the nineteenth-century Treaty Port System.

In the 1890s Britain dominated Hong Kong and its surrounding hinterland, France held a strong position on the Vietnamese border in Yunnan and the southern provinces, Germany held Qingdao and the Russians dominated Manchuria. Following the victory of Japan in the Sino-Japanese War of 1895, Japan came to play an increasingly dominant role among the foreign powers present in the disintegrating Chinese empire. As a result of the war, Japan acquired Taiwan in 1895 and maintained it as a Japanese colony for the next fifty years (which has been, after the American investment in the island, one of the foundations of its economic success in the past thirty years). Japan also began to play a dominant role in the politics of the Korean peninsula and commenced slowly its expansion, both commercial and military, into the Manchurian region. This was the proximate cause of the war between Russia and Japan in 1904–5. At the end of the nineteenth century China was unable to resist these Western and Japanese encroachments on its frontiers and the 'Treaty Ports', conceded under what the Chinese call the 'unequal treaties', were resented as symbols of China's weakness in the face of superior military and naval power.

The only Western-held territories remaining at the present time are, of course, Hong Kong and Macau. Nevertheless, the extraordinary economic success represented by Hong Kong in the 1980s showed to any objective observer that there were also great benefits to China in having a foreign capitalist enclave on its southern coast. Why then should China not grant special conditions to other foreign traders in the late twentieth century, but this time without giving away any national sovereignty or extraterritoriality, maintaining full possession and rights but allowing low tax rates in free trade zones? This was the idea that Premier Zhao put forward in the early 1980s. The actual location of the new special economic zones also echoed the nineteenth-century treaty ports. The Japanese were invited to invest in Dalian, the Taiwanese were attracted to Xiamen (formerly Amoy) and Foochow. China's 'compatriots' in Hong Kong poured capital into the neighbouring special economic zone of Shenzhen, as the Macau investors were drawn to the economic buffer zone of Zhuhai. It was an intelligent and far-sighted strategy which has already benefited China's modernization greatly, although it clearly had its critics at home, among them the more severe ideologues of the communist party. Shenzhen in particular attracted much criticism for its rampant corruption and free-wheeling capitalist lifestyle, epitomized by the booming property market and the small, local stockmarket. However, this policy, based as it was on China's first experience of Western investors a hundred years ago, was a pragmatic response to the need for modernization. It also clearly was a means of keeping Western investors contained in an 'immunization' zone, where they could be controlled and might not infect the rest of the country with their capitalist ideas. In practice, however, this is a difficult policy to enforce. A visitor to the Shenzhen Special Economic Zone might observe the very large crowds of people from the interior provinces who had trekked hundreds of miles to find jobs, paying six times their normal salary on Western goods and services which were clearly unobtainable elsewhere in China.

Western and Japanese investors were also attracted by the large opportunities offered in other provinces with raw materials or energy resources and low labour costs. The average wage in Japan was twenty-seven times that of a Chinese worker. A textile worker in Sichuan was reported to earn $6 a week compared to the equivalent textile worker in one of the poorer American states such as North Carolina where the average was $250 a week. In the final analysis this was the basic business reason for the growing interest of international companies in the Chinese market during the 1980s. The economics of mass production in China were almost irresistible, even taking into account the political risk. To a great extent the corruption, which was endemic to so many small and large business enterprises in China, was seen as lessening this political risk since it involved many of the local party officials in the process. Many observers believed that it was only a matter of time before the Chinese reverted to a more or less open form of free market system, since the reality was that most members of the communist party had a hand in some form of business (up to and including the very highest members of the Politburo in Peking and their families). All of this was again reminiscent of the earlier decades of Western business in China.

In such a vast country as China, where the population is estimated at anywhere between 1.1 and 1.4 billion (the latest 1990 census figures are not widely believed to be accurate), it is very difficult to make any assessment of political risk on a national and regional basis. Each region has its own risks and popular discontents. The success or failure of the Chinese agricultural sector has a great influence on the general political stability of the country. In recent years China has enjoyed a number of years of good harvests and, under the impact of the economic reforms in agriculture, the average income of peasants is reported to have tripled during the 1980s. The most acute discontent that appeared was in the urban populations and particularly among the educated student groups who had benefited little from the reforms and were the victims both of a 30 per cent inflation rate and also of disappointed expectations of reform and openness in the system. Many of them had returned from studying for several years in the West and found that there were few available jobs and no way to use their new-found skills and ideas in the rigid and stultified political system they found in China. Hence the outbreak of popular discontent which culminated in the Tiananmen Square massacre of June 1989. The discontent was really confined to this student group and largely confined to Peking itself and did not draw a national response, least of all from the 800 million peasants who constitute the bulk of the Chinese population.

In the 1990s it may safely be said that the great desire of the majority of the Chinese population, and particularly the younger generation, is for a higher standard of living and a greater choice of consumer goods. These desires come a long way before any vague aspirations towards democracy. One of the newly discovered freedoms which is being enjoyed by many young Chinese is the freedom to travel for the first time even within their own country. The boom in the local Chinese airlines in the last two or three years testifies to this extraordinary surge in internal travel and tourism. Many people in China have money to spend but there are few goods to buy. So travel is one obvious alternative.

The investor considering a project in China should study carefully the joint venture legislation which is the only reasonably coherent body of law available in China today. Although many US and foreign lawyers have laboured hard to help China set up a proper legal system, it cannot be said that the result is yet anywhere near satisfactory. Again, we have to look at Chinese tradition and history to understand why the law has not developed in the same way as in the West. In China the family always comes first and the Confucian obligation overrides that of any legal contract. In earlier times business would only have been done with members of one's own extended family or at least with people whose families were well-known and could, therefore, be pressured to enforce the agreements. Any subject of the emperor being punished for whatever reason, would be punished through his whole family. There was no concept of individual rights but rather the whole family was guilty of the transgressions of the individual.

In the last hundred years the growth of Western business in China has seen a growth of legal contracts, but the respect for these is much less important than the mutual respect of the individuals involved. This is why it is essential for a Westerner doing business with the Chinese, either in China or even in the overseas Chinese communities, to emphasize the personal as much as the legal relationship between the contracting parties. In the long run it is very unusual for any dispute to go to the law courts. Arbitration is always an alternative and preferred route. Hong Kong, because of its strong British legal system may be an exception to this rule but, if we look at the other Confucian societies such as Japan, Taiwan and Korea, it becomes clear that they all have a similar but striking ratio of very few lawyers per head of population. In Japan there are less than 1 per cent of the number of lawyers in the United States. In the whole of Taiwan, with 20 million people, there are only 10,000 lawyers, and yet these two economies are probably the most productive per capita in the world. China follows the same pattern and has very few lawyers and very few people with a knowledge of the law. The political aspect will always override legal contracts, even those with Western or international parties involved.

This then is the first cultural lesson which a Western investor in China must absorb. It is important to do business in the Chinese way, with a great degree of personal trust, and this is also why it is necessary to spend a very long period of time and have a great deal of patience in getting to know your Chinese partner and getting to know his or her objectives and aims in the partnership. At the end of innumerable banquets and tea drinking sessions it is much easier to be sure that each party understands the other on a personal basis and shares a common objective in the joint venture investment. The signing of a legal contract is merely a formal recognition of this personal relationship.

POLITICAL AND ECONOMIC RISK

Chinese history teaches us to expect the unexpected. Mass political movements like the Taiping Rebellion, the Boxer Rebellion and, in more recent years, the Cultural Revolution, have always taken foreign observers by surprise. Changes of dynasty have also occurred unexpectedly as in 1368 and

1644. The final collapse of the empire in 1911 was less unexpected because it had been disintegrating for so long but in the late 1940s nearly all China watchers (with the notable exception of Edgar Snow, the author of *Red Star Over China*) would have predicted that Chiang Kai Shek and the Kuomintang would have held China against the communists (Snow, 1968).

China in the 1990s, with an imminent change of generation at the top, is equally unpredictable. Those who say China is going capitalist probably misunderstand the nature of the whole country which cannot, having over 1 billion people, change so radically. But it is clear, on the other hand, that the communist system, which has been imposed for less than 50 years, is not as deeply imprinted in the minds and hearts of the Chinese people as the older, more enduring, family-centred value system. It is, in the eyes of the younger generation, a failed ideology. The swift collapse of communism in Eastern Europe and increasingly in the Soviet Union shows us how quickly things can change. The political analyst, therefore, will hesitate before making any predictions about China but the trend towards economic reform appears to be firmly set in place. Perhaps the main consideration is that the July 1990 population census of China surprised party officials when the total came out at 1.13 billion rather than 1.08 billion. They had underestimated the numbers of their own people by 50 million (or approximately the whole of the British population!). The one-child policy has not worked, particularly in the countryside. China will have to create 90 million new jobs for young people in the next decade. The central planners who had predicted 4 per cent GNP growth were forced to raise the target to 6 per cent per annum real GNP growth for the rest of the 1990s, otherwise the social consequences of a huge number (some estimates over 100 million) of unemployed youths moving around China between the cities and the countryside would be frightening to contemplate. As a further consequence, China needs more foreign investment and so the open door policy must be maintained. Many of the policies espoused by Zhao Ziyang in the mid-1980s – special economic zones, enterprise reform, bankruptcy law, the development of capital markets, taking party officials out of corporate management – are now making a comeback.

The main priority is now not so much ideological purity but economic growth. China is also responding to the recent but profound change in its relationship with Taiwan which has, for the first time since 1949, dropped the 'three no's' – no communication, no trade, no travel – and ended the political fiction implied by this political assembly of nonagenarian members representing mainland constituencies with the espoused aim of ending the communist rebellion. Taiwan's investment in the mainland is growing rapidly. Over 2,500 companies have now officially registered their PRC capital investments – the total figure may reach US $1 billion. Since June 1989, Taiwan has become easily the most important source of new foreign investment for China. This has obvious political implications. The economic partnership typified by the Taiwanese entrepreneur managing a Hong Kong registered company producing toys with mainland Chinese labour in the special economic zone of Shenzhen has become a very dynamic force.

In the three years 1988 to 1991 China went from zero to a US $15 billion trade surplus with the United States, thus creating for itself overnight the same problem in Washington that Japan had taken thirty years to achieve. In part, of course, this has been due not only to China's dynamic export sector, but also to the freeze on imports in the past two years.

Whoever takes charge of China after Deng Xiaoping will thus inherit a huge economic challenge in providing millions of new jobs and continuing a policy of economic reform without losing political control. The example of Gorbachev in the Soviet Union is a chilling reminder to the Chinese leaders of how easily central control can be lost in such a vast country.

Political risk then in China in the 1990s will depend greatly on the character of the new leadership. It will also vary from region to region and province to province. The southern province of Guangdong and the Pearl River estuary will be closely linked to the success or failure of Hong Kong before and after 1997. The Yangtze River basin, with Shanghai as its natural capital, is likely to assume a greater importance in China's economy (and therefore have more political clout) in the 1990s as the political controls imposed by Peking loosen up. Of course, the possibility of a natural catastrophe can never be discounted, when bearing in mind Chinese history. Although great progress has been made since 1949 in reducing the risk of large scale floods (which used to be a regular occurrence on both the Yangtze and Yellow Rivers), drought and the failure of the harvest can have enormous political and economic consequences.

Again, it is probably true to say that the shift towards the reform policy in agriculture has done a great deal to stabilize and improve China's agricultural yields and production. With the incentive to produce and sell their own crops, the Chinese farmers have enormously increased overall production in the past decade. Essentially, however, the shift towards industrialization of the whole Chinese economy has accelerated greatly in the 1980s. Manufacturing now accounts for 76 per cent of total GNP compared with 24 per cent for agriculture, whereas thirty years ago these figures were 43 per cent and 57 per cent respectively. This has made it significantly easier to predict the course of the Chinese economy. However, China has become much more dependent on foreign trade which now represents over 33 per cent of GNP. Thus the factor of world demand, as opposed to domestic consumer demand, must gradually become more influential. The threat by the United States to remove China's 'most favoured nation' status would cause grave damage to China's booming new export sector, especially in Guangdong province. Therefore, political and economic risk assessment in China are closely intertwined.

INFLATION RISK

Hyperinflation was one of the root causes of the collapse of the Nationalist regime in 1948–9 and this lesson has never been forgotten by the current leadership in Peking. Therefore, with the reappearance of double digit inflation in 1988 in China there was an unhesitating response. The brake was put on money supply and bank lending and overall economic and industrial production at the end of 1988 and this preceded by six months the harsh political repression of June 1989. Although a mild economic recession followed in 1989–90, the Peking government could successfully point to the fact that the inflation rate had been reduced again to single figures (around 5 per cent) by early 1991. At the same time the trend towards rapid growth in consumer imports, which had produced a trade deficit of US $15 billion in 1985 and an average of US $5 billion in the following three years, was reversed and produced a US $9 billion trade surplus in 1990. This was stop-go policy on a huge scale but China's economy responded surprisingly well demonstrating the resilience of its fundamental and dynamic growth. Clearly, however, inflation as a natural barometer remains a very important indicator and if it re-emerges in the 1990s it could be the precursor of further political unrest.

EXCHANGE RATE RISK

China's foreign exchange authorities have begun to adopt a more flexible policy in managing the renmimbi (rmb)/yuan in recent years. Because of their strict adherence to a non-inflationary policy, they had maintained the rmb during the 1970s and early 1980s at an artificially high value against the dollar when compared with the black market rates. After 1988 they began to respond more to the market with progressive devaluations of the Chinese currency, producing a 30 per cent fall in its value over the two years to the end of 1990. In the early months of 1991 the authorities adopted a policy of mini-devaluations or a 'creeping peg' by which the rmb could be devalued progressively in small adjustments by an average factor of 10–15 per cent annually. This had the effect of encouraging exporters while minimizing the impact on domestic inflation. It is likely, therefore, that this policy will continue in the 1990s and that investors can expect a devaluation of at least 10 per cent annually against the dollar.

FOREIGN TRADE RISK

The main risk for foreign businesspeople and investors in China is, as described above, the results of the stop–go economic policy, which continues to result in consumer booms followed by violent clamp downs to cut imports.

However, it is clear that on balance those who take a longer-term approach to selling goods in China will succeed. The overall growth of consumer demand remains very strong and the build up of savings in China is balanced by a newly unleashed propensity to consume many durable goods such as televisions, radios, bicycles, and so on. The sophistication of Chinese consumers, particularly at the top end of the market, should not be underestimated. The number of BMWs and Mercedes Benz sold in the People's Republic can be quite surprising to those who do not know the luxurious tastes of party officials. Perfume, brandy, tobacco and cigars are very successful consumer items just as they are in Hong Kong's duty free shops. Brand name goods in clothing and sports equipment have also begun to secure a very strong foothold in China. As China's export surplus grows so the pressure from trading partners to be able to sell more of these consumer goods and also capital goods will correspondingly increase.

In reality China has only recently made its serious entry as a large player in the world trading system and therefore the world is still feeling the early effects of this entry. Besides, the small proportion of the Chinese population who have so far had access to Western goods indicates how much further this trend has to go. Normally we can expect China to run a significant trade surplus in future years, but much will depend on how its trading relationship with Japan evolves. The Japanese have so far purchased little from China except basic commodities such as crude oil and in turn have invested little in China and, despite occasional successes, have not sold anything like the potential amount of Japanese cars, televisions and other consumer goods that they should be able to achieve in the PRC.

China's place in the world trading system will, therefore, be defined, first, as a leading player in the Asian regional trading bloc and, second, as a significant exporter to North America and Europe.

HONG KONG

Table 5.2 gives details of the overall economic performance of Hong Kong from 1970 to 1990.

POLITICAL RISK

Hong Kong will be handed back by Britain to the People's Republic of China on 1 July 1997. Around this date revolves every question which an investor may ask concerning the risk factors in Hong Kong both before and after 1997. In the last forty years Hong Kong has been transformed from a small British trading port into the third largest international financial and trading centre in the world. This achievement owes much to the British administration and even more to the energy and enterprise of the Hong Kong Chinese

Table 5.2. Economic profile of Hong Kong, 1970–90

	Exchange rate ag. US $	GNP/ GDP growth (%)	CPI	Trade surplus/ (deficit) (US $mn)	P/E	Total turnover (US $mn)	Market year-end closing	Market capital (US $bn)
1970	6.09	9.4	–	–	–	–	211.64	–
1971	5.71	7.3	–	–	–	–	336.86	–
1972	5.70	11.0	–	–	–	–	843.40	–
1973	5.09	12.7	–	–	20.21	–	433.68	–
1974	4.91	2.2	–	–	7.09	274.9	171.11	–
1975	5.03	0.2	–	(723.66)	15.75	2 069.8	350.00	11.28
1976	4.68	17.1	–	(370.94)	16.33	2 840.2	447.67	10.96
1977	4.60	12.5	6.0	(840.87)	12.36	1 423.6	404.02	14.33
1978	4.79	9.5	5.9	(1 909.60)	12.34	6 056.7	495.51	23.55
1979	4.95	11.7	11.9	(2 000.61)	16.68	5 439.4	879.38	22.79
1980	5.10	10.9	15.2	(2 629.02)	20.17	19 945.8	1 473.59	41.13
1981	5.65	9.4	14.1	(2 869.38)	16.00	19 749.0	1 405.82	41.12
1982	6.47	3.0	10.5	(2 397.06)	6.20	6 552.9	783.82	20.35
1983	7.77	6.5	10.0	(1 897.43)	7.68	3 928.6	874.94	18.29
1984	7.81	9.5	8.1	(246.99)	11.79	3 888.4	1 200.38	23.90
1985	7.80	−0.1	3.2	478.59	16.32	7 074.1	1 752.45	34.55
1986	7.79	11.9	2.9	73.81	18.30	15 591.8	2 568.30	53.82
1987	7.77	13.9	5.5	11.07	11.50	47 176.2	2 302.75	54.00
1988	7.80	7.9	7.5	(734.49)	12.40	25 575.2	2 687.44	74.41
1989	7.80	2.3	10.1	990.00	11.50	37 386.6	2 836.57	77.57
1990	7.79	2.5	9.7	(340.95)	10.30	35 016.7	3 024.55	83.49

population, but ultimately also was made possible by the tacit support of China. Hong Kong receives its food and water every day from Guangdong Province. China is also Hong Kong's largest supplier and its second largest export market. Hong Kong has been, at least since 1949, China's window on the world, in the words of Lord Kadoorie, 'it is a neutral point of contact between nations, between East and West (Lord Kadoorie – Sir Elly Kadoorie & Sons in conversation with the author in 1989). As such it is an essential element in world development. We see how and where Hong Kong can benefit China. The measure of our security is how much we can benefit China.' Hong Kong will continue to serve as China's model for modernization.

The 1984 Sino-British Joint Declaration states categorically that the current social and economic systems of Hong Kong will remain unchanged, that Hong Kong will retain the status of an international financial centre and that its markets for foreign exchange, currency, securities and futures will continue. There will be free flow of capital. The Hong Kong dollar will continue to circulate and remain freely convertible.

The above stated policies of China regarding Hong Kong will remain unchanged for fifty years and the socialist system will not be imposed on Hong

Kong. There is a pragmatic basis for this agreement in China's dependency on Hong Kong for it provides vital hard currency and it is a training ground for financial expertise and Western business methods. China also has a large investment in Hong Kong, amounting to more than HK $40 billion (US $5 billion). Hong Kong has been accepted as a full and independent contracting party to the General Agreement of Tariffs and Trade (GATT). It negotiates civil aviation rights independently and has its own shipping register. Hong Kong ranks thirteenth in the world table of trading nations and its container port is now the biggest in the world, larger than New York, Rotterdam and Singapore. It is important that Hong Kong retains its membership, and therefore its quotas in international trade agreements such as the MFA (Multi Fibre Agreement), and retains the most favoured nation (MFN) status for US trade. Given that textiles account for 40 per cent of Hong Kong's exports these quotas are very important for its future prosperity.

There are over 140 international banks operating in Hong Kong. As long as confidentiality and free movement of capital are maintained it is likely that these international banks will use Hong Kong to expand their lending and financing activities in China after 1997. Nevertheless, the Hong Kong and Shanghai Banking Corporation (HSBC), which issues the Hong Kong currency and acts as a *de facto* central bank, has recently moved its legal domicile to the United Kingdom, and the leading trading house in the colony, Jardine Matheson, has moved to Bermuda. It is very easy for any foreign corporation or bank setting up business in Hong Kong to do so through the medium of a Bermudian or other offshore company and, therefore, reduce the risk of China's interference.

The likely business risk in Hong Kong is not the dramatic or obvious risk of the People's Liberation Army marching in one day or the water supply being cut off. The threats are likely to be much more insidious and slow and indeed less visible after 1997 – an increase in taxation, for example, a gradual build up of regulations which would strangle the *laissez-faire* Hong Kong economy and, perhaps more insidious, the gradual spread of corruption which is endemic on the mainland and in Taiwan but which has been tightly controlled by the British authorities through the legal system and the ICAC (Independent Commission Against Corruption).

Another critical factor in Hong Kong's political future will be the question of human rights. No one who has studied the record of the communist party in China can have any confidence in the promises made under the Chinese Constitution or under the 1984 agreement. The communist party has acted ruthlessly in the past to suppress opposition and criticism. Capital punishment is widely used in China for a very broad category of crimes including theft and treason as well as murder. Murder is the only crime for which hanging is technically permitted in Hong Kong, but in practice it has not been used since the 1960s. Martin Lee, the leader of the United Democratic Party in Hong

Kong says, 'we know that human rights are denied on the mainland. It would be folly to pretend human rights will be respected in Hong Kong.' (Martin Lee QC – member of the Legislative Council, Hong Kong, conversation with author 04.01.89). Many Hong Kongers have already voted with their feet and obtained residency and passports in Canada, Australia and the United States. It is estimated that 60,000 people a year are leaving Hong Kong out of a population of 5.86 million. This might not sound too serious but a disproportionate number of emigrants are well-educated with professional skills. This brain drain, however, is offset by the number of people arriving in Hong Kong from elsewhere in the region and also from Britain and the United States, and by the number of Chinese people with Canadian passports, for example, returning to work in the territory where the financial opportunities are far better.

So the delicate balance of confidence in Hong Kong remains subject to occasional buffeting by the winds of change in China. Nevertheless, the resilience of the city was well tested by the events of Tiananmen Square of 4 June 1989. Hong Kong bounced right back, its economy grew and the stockmarket performed well in 1989–90. The territory will be tested again in the future, perhaps in 1992, by further changes in China when the old guard, and particularly Deng Xiaoping, finally disappear. Some predict that the Communist Party will collapse as suddenly as it has in Poland, East Germany, Hungary, Albania, Ethiopia, Mongolia and even now in the Soviet Union. There are very few in China who still believe in the dogma of Marxism and Maoism. The ideology has been exposed as hollow and unable to deliver the living standards which Taiwan and Hong Kong have so obviously succeeded in creating for their people. So there is just an outside chance that China itself will begin to change towards a more liberal and free market system before the date of the handover.

ECONOMIC RISK

Hong Kong's economy which used to be closely linked to the cycles of world trade (as a regional trading centre), since 1980 has become increasingly closely entwined with China's economy. Hence the slowdown in China from late 1988 produced very low GNP growth of 2.3 per cent in 1989 for Hong Kong and 2.5 per cent in 1990. A pick-up in China's demand for foreign goods has an immediate impact on Hong Kong, fueling the growth of re-exports. On the other hand, Hong Kong has a serious problem of labour shortage which has only been partially solved by the transfer or creation of three to four million new jobs in manufacturing across the border in Guangdong Province by Hong Kong manufacturers. At the same time, the number of jobs in Hong Kong's manufacturing industry has fallen from 900,000 to 600,000 in the past decade. Nevertheless, this labour shortage also affects the service sector of the economy and has fueled wage inflation which, in turn, produces an inflationary problem. Hong Kong's consumer price index (CPI) has grown at an average rate of over 10 per cent for the past three years and in 1991 was approaching 14 per cent, the highest in the region. Property prices and rents bear the brunt of this increase whereas food prices, for example, are fairly stable and depend more on imports from China.

The one stable factor in all this is the peg, or fixed link, of the Hong Kong dollar to the US dollar since October 1983. The value of the Hong Kong dollar was fixed at 7.8 to 1 US dollar and has remained at that rate ever since. Hence the Hong Kong economic and financial cycle has been closely linked to that of the US dollar and US economy. Hong Kong interest rates follow US interest rates up and down. A weak US dollar has tended to be good for Hong Kong's exports and vice versa. Hong Kong generally runs a small trade deficit but it is dependent on the vagaries of the China trade. On the other hand, Hong Kong's trade surplus with the United States has been reduced because much of its garment, toy and shoe exports have been redirected from China to the United States.

An investment in Hong Kong is already an investment in China with all the risks and the potential of that vast but unpredictable nation. On the other hand, for many Western companies the familiar British legal and commercial system, which will be maintained in Hong Kong after 1997, is a reassuring entry pad into China and indeed Hong Kong remains the preferred Asia Pacific regional headquarters for most US and European companies. Japan has also been a very important investor in Hong Kong with almost US $3 billion invested since 1989.

Which other Asian city can or could replace Hong Kong? This is a critical, strategic question asked by many Western investors and companies. Tokyo remains very much enclosed within the powerful Japanese economy and culture and does not have the same international character. There is the basic question of language, whereby it is more difficult to obtain financial and commercial information in English. This is a problem also afflicting Taipei which has remained intrinsically Chinese in its legal and cultural system. Seoul is a tightly controlled market, difficult for Westerners to penetrate. Bangkok has communication and transport problems, notably the traffic, which will take at least ten years to solve. The only really viable alternative to Hong Kong remains Singapore. Its economic structure is built on trade and finance and its labour is mainly highly educated Chinese. Its stock exchange ranks fourth in the region, behind Hong Kong which is in third place, and its futures exchange is second only to Tokyo's. Singapore offers an attractive tax structure of 10 per cent for companies choosing it as an operational headquarters. None the less, it has a chronic labour shortage and its government controlled economy remains rigid and highly regulated, so that the Singapore dollar, for example, has not been allowed to develop into an international currency. On balance, however, it is an attractive place in which to live and to operate and may well be the choice of companies which perceive the political risk in Hong Kong after 1997 as being too great. However, the reward side of those who can seize the opportunity of using Hong Kong as a regional base or even more as a base to penetrate the China market will be very considerable. Nowhere is the risk reward ratio so finely balanced as in Hong Kong. Nowhere perhaps is the gamble more worth taking.

JAPAN

Table 5.3 gives details of the overall economic performance of Japan from 1970 to 1990.

Table 5.3. Economic profile of Japan, 1970–90

	Exchange rate ag. US $	GNP/ GDP growth (%)	CPI	Trade surplus/ (deficit) (US $bn)	P/E	Total turnover (US $mn)	Market year-end closing	Market capital (US $bn)
1970		8.1					1 987.14	
1971		5.2					2 713.74	
1972	302.00	9.0	4.2			70 977	5 207.94	
1973	280.00	4.7	11.56			53 230	4 306.80	
1974	300.95	−0.2	23.20			41 170	3 817.22	
1975	305.15	4.0	11.87			51 011	4 358.60	
1976	292.80	4.0	9.38			80 813	4 987.47	
1977	240.00	4.8	8.19			89 584	4 865.60	
1978	194.60	5.1	4.21			167 186	6 001.85	
1979	239.70	5.5	3.72			145 645	6 569.73	
1980	203.00	3.2	7.74		20.4	179 752	7 063.13	360.6
1981	219.90	3.2	4.97	19.96	21.1	224 486	7 681.84	399.7
1982	235.00	3.7	2.74	18.08	25.8	155 623	8 016.67	398.3
1983	232.20	2.8	1.89	31.46	34.7	236 196	9 893.62	514.6
1984	251.10	4.6	2.26	44.26	37.9	270 705	11 542.60	616.5
1985	200.50	4.8	2.04	55.99	35.2	392 574	13 083.18	910.7
1986	159.10	2.8	0.62	92.82	47.3	1 004 627	18 820.64	1 741.0
1987	123.50	5.1	0.03	96.42	58.3	2 030 259	21 564.00	2 634.8
1988	125.85	5.8	0.75	95.00	58.4	2 268 742	30 159.00	3 677.4
1989	143.45	4.8	2.28	76.89	70.6	2 319 502	38 915.87	4 119.2
1990	134.40	5.0	3.13	63.86	29.0	1 316 220	23 848.71	2 716.5

POLITICAL RISK

Japan always has the highest score in the world for political stability and economic potential and the lowest score for risk. Yet the approach of analyzing country risk through an historical perspective suggests that the picture may be more complex than that. At several times in Japan's history foreigners have been totally excluded, for instance, during the Tokogawa period of 1640 to 1853. Although on the surface Japan, since 1945, has been one of the most open of all Asian countries to Western residents, investors and ideas, the underlying society and culture has proved remarkably resilient and resistant to change. Nowhere is this clearer than in the political life of Japan which on the surface appears to be a modern democracy with opposing political parties and ideologies. The underlying reality, however, is that the Liberal Democratic Party (LDP) has held power consistently for the past forty years, even though prime ministers have recently changed on average every two years and different factions have held sway within the ruling party. At no time has it seemed likely that the Japan Socialist Party, the leading opposition group, would take power or that Japan's basic pro-business and growth policies would be altered in any way.

The real power, it has often been said, lies with the officials of the ministries, particularly the Ministry of International Trade and Industry (MITI) and the Ministry of Finance (MOF). These ministries constitute the models of long-term economic planning which have inspired a number of other countries, for example, Thailand.

Political stability, then, has been remarkable in Japan in the post-war period but, if we take a longer view of Japan's history, it is by no means certain that this situation is likely to be maintained in the future. Much will depend on the continued success of the Japanese economy to see whether there would be unpopular discontent or a serious opposition challenge to the LDP's continued rule. The Japanese constitution continues to be pacifist and to enshrine the principle of constitutional monarchy. The smooth succession of the Emperor Akihito after the death of the longest reigning Emperor in Japan's history, Hirohito, was testament to this enduring and stable constitutional system. Japanese politics also are, as elsewhere, intimately involved with the world of finance. Much of the corruption and scandals of recent years, which have led to the resignation of three prime ministers in the past five years, have stemmed from the frequent involvement of politicians in the Tokyo stockmarket. All of this is accepted by most Japanese as a normal way of life for politicians, for whom there is not, in any case, a vast popular respect.

Political risk in Japan, as elsewhere, is closely entwined with economic factors. The political stability that Japan has enjoyed since 1960 is certainly, in part, the result of Japan's tremendous economic success. The Liberal Democratic Party has been able to satisfy the broad, popular demands of the Japanese people and of its rural constituents, in particular, by recycling growing government tax revenues into ambitious infrastructure projects in various favoured prefectures. A classic case was, of course, Prime Minister Tanaka in the early 1970s who was the author of the 'rebuilding the archipelago' policy and who was able to direct billions of yen to his home prefecture of Niigata for hospitals, schools, roads, tunnels and national projects which created employment opportunities. Therefore, the continued success of the Japanese economy and the export machine of 'Japan Inc.' means that the LDP's pre-eminence is unlikely to be challenged, certainly not by Japan's socialist party.

The predictability and continuance of pro-business policies in Japan are a vital factor in its industrial growth. Most of these policies are in any case directed not by Japanese politicians but by the all-powerful ministries – of finance, of trade and MITI. The factors which would offset this smooth political stability in Japan are more likely to be external shocks, such as US trade protectionist measures or a sudden rise in the price of energy or political instability in Japan's largest neighbours such as China and the Soviet Union. All these events, however, have been well planned for as has the possibility of another great Tokyo earthquake. Japan's exports have been diversified more and more widely and the dependence on the United States reduced. Japan's military spending has, in fact, been higher than is widely appreciated overseas and Japan has a low profile but efficient navy.

The ease with which Japan was able to cope with the jump in oil prices, from US $20 to US $40 per barrel, during the recent Gulf War showed both the sense of long-term planning, high inventories and the efficiency with which Japan uses energy to produce GNP growth, a ratio which has improved dramatically over the past twenty years. So, despite its apparent vulnerability Japan has intelligently used its scarce natural resources and its major human resources to create a stable and planned future for its people.

ECONOMIC RISK

The economic risk in Japan is also, for the same reasons, less than it may appear to be to outside observers. Japan's dependence on imports for all its vital daily necessities (except for rice) has been converted into a strength as a result of the virtuous circle of export surpluses and a strong yen. In addition, the fall in commodity prices, not only oil but also minerals and foodstuffs, has improved Japan's terms of trade. This is particularly true in relation to its trading partners such as Australia where the steep fall of the Australian dollar against the yen and the collapse of wool, meat and metal prices has benefited Japan and weakened Australia. Of course, all these trends can go into reverse and in the 1970s Japan had to cope with high inflation, high commodity prices and a weaker yen. The shift, after 1985, from an export oriented economy to an economy which depended for more than 60 per cent of its growth on domestic consumer spending and capital expenditure by both corporations and by government, has produced a less volatile and more stable growth pattern. Japanese consumers in particular have developed more and more sophisticated tastes for foreign imports, whether BMWs, Mercedes Benz',

French wines and perfumes or American beef and coca cola. The entertainment budget of Japanese corporations alone is larger than the GNP of many developing countries. Given the conservatism of most Japanese salaried men (and, more particularly, of their wives who control the purse strings) and the high savings rate which this engenders, it is impressive to realise that despite this high spending on consumer items and entertainment there is still a strong financial backing behind Japan's economic system.

Compared with the consumer debt of Americans, Japanese consumers typically have large amounts of their savings on deposit in banks and only 2 per cent of their assets are held in shares on the Tokyo stockmarket. Thus the fall in the Tokyo stockmarket has had very little effect on the overall health of the economy. Japanese consumers have also shown a growing appetite for foreign travel and when we consider that only 10 per cent of the Japanese population have so far travelled overseas it is clear that there is still a considerable growth potential for the tourist industry. This is one of the ways in which Japan can recycle its trade and current account surplus. Japan has, therefore, created an enviable stability and strength in its economy and financial system which is able to withstand most external shocks.

The yen is, however, more volatile than most other Asian currencies since it trades freely against the US dollar and European currencies in the large and highly liquid foreign exchange markets in London, New York and Tokyo. Every other currency – Hong Kong dollar, Singapore dollar, Malaysian ringgit, Thai baht, Korean won, New Taiwan dollar, and so on – is controlled or managed by the national central bank and is usually, therefore, held in a peg or managed appreciation or depreciation against the dollar. The yen, by contrast, can move by up to 5 per cent in a single day. This is, therefore, the largest single risk which investors in Japan can run on a short-term basis. In addition, the factors that move the yen may be quite exogenous to Japan itself. A rise or fall in employment indicators or the trade deficit in the United States can, for example, influence the dollar, and thus the yen parity, far more than any economic indicators. The co-ordination of the G7 or G3 (comprising the United States, Germany and Japan) has at times been close, but at other times it appears that the central banks in Washington, Bonn and Tokyo have divergent aims. At one moment, the Federal Reserve in Washington may be trying to promote economic recovery and boost employment while the Bank of Japan in Tokyo and the Bundesbank in Germany may be trying to restrain inflation.

Given that in the past Japan's rate of economic growth has been considerably higher than in the United States, money supply has also been allowed to expand at a higher rate and, therefore, the clamp down on monetary growth and bank lending in Japan has come at a very late stage in the economic cycle. For the purposes of this book, however, we shall try to take a longer-term approach and predict that the yen will, indeed, resume its long-term path of appreciation against the US dollar for all the sound fundamental reasons which have propelled it from its post-war fixed parity of 360 yen to the dollar, between 1948 and 1971, to its recent high of 120 yen at the end of 1989. Despite the strength in the dollar in 1991 it appears unlikely that the yen will fall much below 150 yen and the long-term purchasing power parity would indicate that the yen would approach and even surpass a level of 100 yen to the dollar during the 1990s. It is rumoured that the Bank of Japan would take advantage of this situation to remonetize the yen, in other words, to divide its value by 100 and achieve the national virility symbol of having 1 yen equal 1 dollar. Therefore, the long-term view of the yen remains extremely positive.

INFLATION AND TRADE RISKS

Inflation in Japan has been held to single digits ever since 1975. In fact, during the 1980s it has rarely exceeded 3 per cent and hence the yen has benefited from its relatively low level of price increases compared with its major trading competitors. It is, therefore, reasonable to expect that the inflation rate in Japan will be held at very low levels during the 1990s, averaging around 2 per cent per annum. What happens to Japan's trade surplus is a question of global proportions and consequences. Although the overall figure peaked in 1987, just short of US $100 billion, and has fallen since to a level of about US $60 billion in 1990, it is apparent that the strength of Japan's exporters is a long-term phenomenon which is not likely to be seriously challenged for the next decade. However, it is important to note that during the US recession in 1990–1 Japan succeeded in maintaining a high export surplus by redirecting sales of capital goods towards the Asian region in particular, led by Korea and Taiwan. The restraints which are likely to be imposed by the European Community (EC) on the growth of Japan's car imports into the EC will also pose a challenge for Japan as similar actions by the United States in the early 1980s forced Japan to reconsider its trade and investment policies. Increasingly it is apparent that the response of Japanese companies is to move production offshore and thus to reduce the visible trade surplus. In fact, it has been predicted that by the year 2000, 50 per cent of Japan's imports will be coming from Japanese owned plants in overseas countries, particularly in places such as Thailand, which will produce cheap electronic goods, miniature ball bearings, textiles, canned food, televisions and many other items which were formerly produced within Japan itself. For truly global companies such as Sony, Matsushita and Honda, therefore, the overall effect will still be very positive even though 70 per cent of their production and sales is outside Japan itself. Japan's trade surplus may very gradually shrink during the 1990s as this phenomenon of overseas production and worldwide corporate investment increases. Nissan's plan to produce cars in the north of England and sell them in the European Community has been challenged by the French but in the long term this is the only strategy that can work for a Japanese company wishing to penetrate the new single European market.

For a long-term economic analyst, therefore, it makes sense to try to combine analysis of Japan's trade position with the direction of its capital flows and corporate investment plans.

TAIWAN

Table 5.4 gives details of the overall economic performance of Taiwan from 1970 to 1990.

Table 5.4. Economic profile of Taiwan, 1970–90

	Exchange rate ag. US $	GNP/ GDP growth (%)	CPI	Trade surplus/ (deficit) (US $mn)	P/E	Total turnover (US $mn)	Market year-end closing	Market capital (US $bn)
1970	40.00	11.3	3.60	(42.6)		271.7	123.38	0.42
1971	40.00	13.0	2.80	216.5		590.0	135.13	0.52
1972	40.00	13.4	3.00	474.6		1 351.3	228.03	0.75
1973	37.95	12.8	8.20	690.9		2 294.9	495.45	2.26
1974	38.00	1.2	47.50	(1 326.7)		1 147.0	193.06	1.33
1975	38.00	4.4	5.20	(642.9)		3 430.0	330.08	1.95
1976	38.00	13.7	2.50	567.4		3 841.0	372.20	2.49
1977	38.00	10.3	7.00	849.8		4 531.0	450.00	3.19
1978	36.00	14.0	5.80	1 660.2		10 046.0	532.43	4.27
1979	36.03	8.5	9.80	1 329.7		5 703.2	549.55	4.97
1980	36.01	7.1	19.00	77.5		4 501.9	558.45	6.09
1981	37.84	5.8	16.30	1 411.6		5 529.0	551.03	5.33
1982	39.91	4.1	3.00	3 315.9		3 354.4	443.57	5.10
1983	40.27	8.6	1.40	4 835.6		9 035.1	761.92	7.61
1984	39.47	11.6	−0.02	8 497.3		8 220.8	838.07	9.90
1985	39.85	5.6	−0.20	10 624.0		4 899.1	835.12	10.45
1986	35.50	12.6	0.70	15 684.0	15.3	19 032.6	1 039.11	15.45
1987	28.55	11.9	0.50	18 581.2	28.7	93 472.3	2 339.86	48.46
1988	28.17	7.8	1.30	10 929.0	68.9	279 305.1	5 119.11	120.10
1989	26.17	7.3	4.40	13 937.5	92.0	970 881.2	9 624.18	232.05
1990	27.00	5.2	4.10	12 490.0	36.4	744 599.0	4 530.16	100.63

Taiwan is the most invisible country on the planet. On many people's maps it does not exist. In fact, Taiwan is recognized by only twenty-two countries, mostly small island states like itself in the South Pacific and the Caribbean. And yet it is an oriental paradox – it has a financial and diplomatic influence which is out of all proportion to its small size. For historical and cultural reasons Taiwan stands between China and Japan. (The slow pace of the Sino-Japanese relationship since 1972 may be partly caused by this conundrum.)

Indeed, if Taiwan is now going to be brought back into the fold it is also reasonable to expect the level of Japanese investment and trade in China to accelerate. It is very probable that Japan will use Taiwan as a 'middle-man' for trade and investment in China.

Taiwan is dependent on its close relationship with the United States and its very successful diplomacy and public relations campaign which, ever since Madame Chiang Kai-Shek's days in the 1940s (so well described in *The Soong Dynasty*, Seagrave, 1985), has sustained a high level of sympathy in Washington for the Nationalist regime. Taiwan also has close relations with South Africa, from which it buys essential raw materials such as coal, and also with Israel, with whom it has had military as well as trade links.

For all these reasons, much of the real Taiwan has been hidden for many years. It is misunderstood by Westerners – the country has been the most difficult of all Asian countries to follow and understand. However, since the lifting of martial law in 1987 much of this has changed. People in Taipei are again willing to talk openly and it is possible to begin to understand the sense in which Taiwan has become a repository of much of the best of the old Chinese traditions. Readers of Lin Yutang (1942) will recognize that there are many other facets to the Chinese way of life than the Maoist totalitarianism which had come to be the way the world saw China in the 1960s and 1970s. In Taiwan can be found many of the old Chinese arts – a strong family life, Confucianism, a flourishing trade in traditional Chinese medicines, the martial arts, an excellent standard of Chinese movies and television, and the tradition of Chinese law.

Nevertheless, the basic geopolitical fact about Taiwan is that it sits under the shadow of mainland China and under the threat of reunification, whether peaceful or by military means. There is no doubt that in the last few years and especially since June 1989, the elderly leadership of the Communist Party in Peking and the similarly elderly leaders of the Kuomintang (KMT) in Taipei have begun, for the first time since 1949, to have serious talks and regular communication. At the same time the flow of investment from Taiwan into mainland China, especially into the neighbouring province of Fujian, has grown dramatically and the two-way trade is now approaching US $4 billion annually. In the early days of this two-way business, the authorities in Taipei turned a blind eye to the many small projects that Taiwanese businesspeople were embarking upon with PRC partners. Much of the business went through Hong Kong anyway and so could be disguised. Also, there was an enormous increase in the number of annual visitors from Taiwan into China, many of whom were old KMT soldiers revisiting their ancestral villages and relatives on the mainland. (The actual numbers of Taiwanese visitors going through Hong Kong rose to about 1.3 million in 1990). Along with the travel and tourism came the investment and it is now estimated that there is over US $500 million of direct Taiwanese capital in plants and small businesses in

China. Many of the most successful toy and electronics factories in Shenzhen, across the border from Hong Kong, are owned and managed by Taiwanese. Speaking Mandarin or the Fujianese dialect, they have the same natural advantage in dealing with mainland officials and businesspeople that the Hong Kong Cantonese have with the inhabitants of Guangdong Province.

So the analysis of risk and reward in Taiwan must already take account of this rapidly growing economic integration between Taiwan and China which, by the end of the 1990s, will probably mean that over 30 per cent of Taiwan's trade is with the mainland and that the total investment from Taiwan to China may approach US $5 billion or even US $10 billion. As with Hong Kong, increasingly an investment in Taiwan will be seen indirectly as a 'play' or an investment in China itself. Nevertheless, Taiwan remains a free capitalist enclave with some very successful entrepreneurial and export-oriented companies. The government's role in the economy is relatively small. It has pursued consistently, since 1950, a *laissez-faire* policy which allows small family run companies typically to change their product line every two or three years to meet the demands of American or other international clients. The black market sector of the Taiwanese economy is estimated to exceed 60 per cent of the total, hence all statistics about the economy are somewhat suspect. However, they clearly indicate that the export strengths, which have powered the Taiwanese economic boom for thirty or forty years, remain intact despite the shortage of skilled labour, the high cost of labour and the strong New Taiwan dollar, which has impelled many Taiwanese businesspeople to shift their production to Thailand, the Philippines, and Malaysia as well as China. (None the less, the best measure of Taiwan's economic success is in its US $75 billion of foreign exchange reserves, the second highest in the world after Japan.)

What then is the real risk to Taiwan? After Hong Kong is taken over in 1997 Taiwan will appear more isolated and it will have lost its neutral meeting point with China which the British colony has represented. On the other hand, by that time Taiwan and China may have grown sufficiently close in economic, if not in political, terms that Hong Kong will have become unnecessary. Direct flights between Taipei and Xiamen or Shanghai will soon become a reality. Direct trade and investment are already commencing. Some form of political agreement allowing for Taiwan's autonomy, if not independence, may be worked out. It will be a 'Chinese solution' – face will be saved. The 'one country two systems' formula applied to Hong Kong and Macau was always designed by Peking with the objective of regaining Taiwan in the long term. That long term may not be as long as some observers have predicted. The passing away of the older generation who fought in the bitter civil wars between the communists and the KMT from 1927 to 1949 will remove much of the bitterness and open up the way for a new dialogue between the younger leaders in the two Chinas.

The strongest argument for a political compromise and a formula for coexistence is the natural complementarity of the two Chinese communities on an economic basis. China has the labour, the land and the resources. Taiwan has the capital, the technology and the trained entrepreneurs. A formidable Chinese Economic Community (CEC) may well be in the making and could be a reality before the end of the century. This is the rosy scenario. However, a more pessimistic view would be to see a return to ideological extremism in Peking resulting in a renewed cold war across the Taiwan Straits, a cut off of business and cultural links, and a potential military conflict. Even in this very gloomy scenario Taiwan may be able to defend itself and maintain its economic prosperity because it will still have the economic support of both Japan and the United States.

The risks for an investor in the Taipei stockmarket are specifically those of a highly priced and highly volatile securities market with very weak regulations and poor accounting standards. It was once estimated that, out of 140 listed companies in Taiwan, perhaps twenty or thirty counters were those of companies which were technically bankrupt. In the casino-like atmosphere of the Taipei stock exchange, daily volumes frequently exceed US $1 billion and a local investor (probably a housewife, taxi driver or factory worker) may buy shares in the morning to sell them back in the afternoon or even trade five or six times a day, since the brokerage commissions are only 0.1 per cent. These investors take little account of security analysis or of the investment fundamentals which might count more for long-term Western investors. The speculative atmosphere of the Taipei exchange does, therefore, portray a high degree of risk. However, the New Taiwan (NT) dollar is a very steady currency in relation to the US dollar. The economy of the island has shown a steady and non-inflationary growth rate and savings are very high in relation to disposable income. Hence there is a lot of available cash in the system for investment.

The most important risk to consider for a Western investor trying to get into the Taiwanese market is the choice of a trustworthy and reliable local partner. This is much more difficult to achieve in Taiwan than in, say, Hong Kong, where the British legal and commercial system and the educational system are more familiar. Taiwan has a purely Chinese culture and way of life even though most of the younger businesspeople are educated in the universities of the United States and many have PhDs. Nevertheless, the way of doing business remains a traditional Chinese way. Therefore, nothing can be achieved by means of legal contracts or agreements in the accepted Western sense. Even more than in China, Taiwan depends on the personal contact and trust between the two individuals involved. Many Western banks have come to grief in their pursuit of the elusive Taiwan millionaires in the private banking sector and in their corporate loans to apparently sound Taiwanese companies, which either cannot or will not repay. Recourse is very hard to enforce and the legal system is, frankly, primitive. These are the major risks in doing business in Taiwan but the potential rewards should not be underestimated. Those who have had a long-term commitment to the island republic, have had good contacts with the government and have done business in the Chinese way with a good local Chinese partner have been able to demonstrate very good long-term returns on their investments. In addition, the links that Taiwan businesspeople have built around the globe, in the United States in particular but also increasingly in Canada, where they have followed Hong Kong investors into British Columbia, in Australia, in the Philippines and in Bangkok, are impressive.

This was an impoverished island in 1949 with a sudden influx of nearly 2 million immigrants from the mainland. There were no natural resources and no significant overseas support, only the protection of the US military. Taiwan is an even more extraordinary economic miracle in some respects than Japan because of its sheer hard work, and dependence on brains and education, and entrepreneurial flexibility, to produce what the world wants and to sell it worldwide.

KOREA

Table 5.5 gives details of the overall economic performance of Korea from 1970 to 1990.

POLITICAL RISK

Political volatility has characterized the history of South Korea (referred to as Korea throughout this section) during the past forty years, while at the same time an extraordinary economic boom has occurred. The historical analysis of Korea in Chapter 3 confirmed its very strong Confucian and authoritarian past. The same rigid discipline has been characteristic of the military government under President Park during the 1960s and 1970s, which were the most successful decades in economic terms particularly in the growth of Korea's exports and in the per capita income. It is important to remember how completely the cities and transport system of the southern part of the Korean peninsula had been destroyed in the civil war of the 1950s. The effort of reconstruction was, therefore, enormous. Living standards in the 1960s were extremely low. The threat from North Korea has exerted a continuous military pressure on the South in the past forty years which is probably unique to any country in the world, even including West Germany or Taiwan. Seoul is only 30 kilometres from the demilitarized zone and, therefore, lives in a continuous state of tension and fear of an imminent invasion. This very real threat is also translated into a very high percentage of military spending in the national budget. If Korea is compared with Japan, the Koreans have had to spend ten times more of their national income on defence than the Japanese and yet have succeeded in recording higher rates of economic growth.

Table 5.5. Economic profile of Korea, 1970–90

	Exchange rate ag. US $	GNP/ GDP growth (%)	CPI	Trade surplus/ (deficit) (US $mn)	P/E	Total turnover (US $mn)	Market year-end closing	Market capital (US $bn)
1970	–	8.8	–	–		–	–	
1971	373.20	9.2	13.5	(1 046)		24	–	
1972	398.90	5.9	11.5	(574)		72	–	
1973	397.50	14.4	3.2	(566)		144	–	
1974	484.00	7.9	24.5	(1 937)		168	–	
1975	484.00	6.5	25.2	(1 671)		312	89.7	
1976	484.00	13.2	15.3	(591)		600	104.0	
1977	484.00	10.9	10.0	(477)		1 296	137.0	
1978	484.00	10.9	14.5	(1 781)		1 656	144.9	6.0
1979	484.00	7.4	18.2	(4 396)		1 272	119.0	5.4
1980	659.90	−3.0	28.7	(4 384)	2.6	1 080	106.9	3.8
1981	700.50	7.4	21.6	(3 628)	3.1	2 424	131.4	4.2
1982	748.80	5.7	7.1	(2 594)	3.4	1 872	127.3	4.4
1983	795.50	10.9	3.4	(1 764)	4.9	1 656	121.2	4.4
1984	827.40	8.6	2.3	(1 036)	8.0	2 976	142.5	6.2
1985	890.20	5.4	2.5	(19)	12.0	3 432	163.4	7.4
1986	861.40	12.9	2.8	4 206	12.8	9 168	272.6	13.9
1987	792.30	13.0	3.0	7 659	19.8	21 552	525.1	33.0
1988	684.10	12.4	7.1	11 445	26.2	69 408	907.2	94.3
1989	677.40	6.7	5.7	4 597	23.3	103 200	909.7	140.9
1990	714.60	8.6	9.5	1 433	17.4	63 360	696.1	110.2

The fierce political in-fighting, which has been a constant characteristic of Korean history, was suppressed for a period in the 1970s and 1980s, both before and after the assassination of President Park. Since 1987 the opening up of the democratic process has been smoothly handled despite the continuing student riots and disturbances. In fact, stockmarket investors have generally ignored the television images of riot police, tanks firing tear gas and students throwing petrol bombs, to concentrate more on the continuous success of Korean companies in their conquest of overseas export markets and their impressive earnings growth. Nevertheless, the threat from the North and the fierceness of the Korean political opposition do combine to give Korea a lower score for political stability than its neighbours. We have the sense in Korea of a higher risk but also a much greater potential should the *rapprochement* with the North lead to a peaceful reunification. The economic potential of such a reunified peninsula is described in the final chapter of this book.

One factor that will come into play in the 1990s will be the possible withdrawal of American troops. Just as North Korea will face its moment of truth with the death of Kim Il Sung and the gradual withdrawal of both Soviet and Chinese support for its economy, so too South Korea will find itself increasingly standing alone. Whether they like it or not, the Koreans will have to face the fact that Japan will play a vital role both in the economic and political spheres. The history of the peninsula also suggests that the great powers including not only China and Japan, but also the United States and the Soviet Union, will maintain their vested interests as far as they can in the peninsula.

ECONOMIC RISK

South Korea has the highest overall score for economic growth in the world over the past twenty years even when compared with the other Asian tigers. The average growth over a twenty-year period has been close to 9 per cent in real terms, at certain times reaching even 13–14 per cent. This means that the average Korean today has a per capita income of nearly US $6,000 per annum, an income which has grown nearly thirty times in thirty years. There have been tremendous social changes resulting from this economic boom, notably the shift of population from the countryside into the cities and the shift in the economic structure from agriculture to industry and, more recently, to the service sector. This has all occurred in a shorter period of time than in almost any other advanced economy. What took England one hundred years and Japan thirty years, has taken Korea typically less than ten years. There has been some slowing during the 1980s compared to the 1970s, but in 1991 Korea still scores the highest overall rating for GNP growth. Its industrial workforce has not lost its competitive edge and the average working week in Korea is still in excess of fifty hours, the longest working week in the world. These are the foundations of Korea's continued economic success. It is unlikely that such characteristics, being social in origin, will disappoint us in the next decade. Therefore it is reasonable to expect Korea's economy to continue to be one of Asia's most successful.

The flexibility of its large trading companies, the *chaebol*, has been recently underlined again as they have shifted their emphasis from the United States, Canada and Europe towards the new markets of China and the Soviet Union. There is little doubt that Korean exporters will be leading the Japanese in providing Russian consumers with basic consumer goods. The readiness to take risks in new areas has continuously paid off for Korean companies just as it did when they were able to grab the major construction contracts in the Middle East during the oil boom of the 1970s. (These new trade links have also translated into new diplomatic links with China, Hungary, Poland and the Soviet Union, thus further isolating North Korea from its communist neighbours.)

INFLATION RISK

Inflation in Korea has been higher than in Japan or Taiwan. In the 1970s,

Korea experienced an annual average inflation rate of nearly 15 per cent. Beginning in 1982, however, the tight monetary policy succeeded in bringing this annual consumer price index down to single digits until 1990 when the rate jumped again to 9.5 per cent. The Korean export boom has led to a big inflow of foreign exchange accompanying Korea's trade surpluses of the past five years. This, in turn, has led to a sharp increase in money supply and a boom in real estate prices in Seoul. Thus the rise of both the Korean share market and property market since 1985 has in a sense been a lagging indicator of the economic boom of earlier years with its inevitable build up of national and personal wealth among the Korean population. Nowhere has the number of investors grown faster than in the Seoul stockmarket during the 1980s. Thus rising prices have reflected rising national wealth. This inflation problem has been, and can again be, tamed by a strong central bank response and this is what we would expect in the 1990s.

EXCHANGE RATE RISK

The exchange rate of the Korean won against the US dollar has reflected both the relative inflation rates of Korea and its international trading partners and also the more recent success of Korea in repaying much of its foreign debt and building up its reserves. The won was held very steady during the 1970s and then allowed to devalue between 1980 and 1985 from 484 won to the dollar to its lowest level of 890 won to the dollar. With the sharp improvement in Korea's overseas trade position the won started to appreciate from 1986 onwards and reached a high of 650 to the dollar in 1989. With the subsequent relapse of Korea into a new trade deficit in 1990 and the recovery of the dollar in world exchange markets, the Korean won has again depreciated slightly. However, there is a high degree of stability and the currency is managed by the central bank. We should, therefore, not expect a devaluation of more than 5 per cent per annum unless Korea's trade or inflation problems worsen significantly.

It is likely that Korea's foreign trade position will improve again thanks to the country's competitive position in export markets. In a more liberated domestic economy with lower tariffs on foreign goods, however, it will be more difficult to restrain the growth of imports as Korean consumers demand a greater choice. Korea's main deficit is with Japan and consists largely of capital goods. This is likely to continue as long as Korean manufacturers wish to maintain their competitive edge in the most modern plant and equipment.

THAILAND

Table 5.6 gives details of the overall economic performance of Thailand from 1970 to 1990.

Table 5.6. Economic profile of Thailand, 1970–90

	Exchange rate ag. US $	GNP/ GDP growth (%)	CPI	Trade surplus/ (deficit) (US $mn)	P/E	Total turnover (US $mn)	Market year-end closing	Market capital (US $bn)
1970		10.5						
1971		5.0						
1972	20.927 5	4.1	4.8					
1973	20.375 0	9.9	15.4					
1974	20.375 0	4.4	24.4					
1975	20.400 0	4.8	5.5		5.0	27.5	84.08	0.26
1976	20.400 0	9.4	4.1		5.8	48.5	82.70	0.36
1977	20.400 0	9.9	7.6		11.3	1 288.2	181.59	0.94
1978	20.390 0	10.4	7.9		8.5	2 798.9	257.73	1.62
1979	20.425 0	5.3	9.8		5.8	1 099.1	149.40	1.39
1980	20.630 0	4.8	19.8		6.4	317.5	124.67	1.24
1981	23.000 0	6.3	12.7		9.5	109.6	106.62	1.02
1982	23.000 0	4.1	5.3		11.8	255.7	123.50	1.28
1983	23.000 0	7.3	3.7		6.5	396.5	134.47	1.51
1984	27.150 0	7.1	0.9		7.2	390.4	142.29	1.75
1985	26.650 0	3.5	2.4		9.6	575.2	134.95	1.86
1986	26.130 0	4.5	1.8	(0.4)	12.3	956.4	207.20	2.88
1987	25.070 0	8.4	2.5	(1.4)	9.3	4 872.0	284.99	5.51
1988	25.240 0	12.0	3.9	(4.3)	12.0	6 198.9	386.73	8.86
1989	25.690 0	12.2	5.4	(5.5)	26.4	14 676.1	879.19	25.67
1990	25.290 0	10.0	6.0	(8.8)	13.8	24 801.5	612.86	24.26

POLITICAL RISK

The historical analysis in Chapter 3 has highlighted Thailand's uniqueness in South East Asia in escaping the colonial experience and maintaining its freedom and independence. In addition it has been shown how the monarchy played a key role in the nineteenth century in maintaining the country's political stability and independence. It is, nevertheless, sobering to realize that since the absolute monarchy was ended in 1932 there have been no less than twenty-one *coup d'etats*, of which twelve have been successful. The recent international perception of Thailand was very much coloured by the experience of the past fifteen years as there had been no successful *coup d'etat* since 1977. Thus the one that took place in February 1991 was a surprise to many foreign observers and investors, although it had broad popular support and the tacit blessing of King Bhumibol himself. The army was felt to be acting not only to further its own cause but to stamp out political corruption and restore, within a period of six months, a democratically elected government. The Cabinet, which was put in place immediately after this coup, contained fifteen PhDs out of a total of twenty-three ministers, and the

generals were in a small minority compared to the businesspeople, diplomats
and civil servants with a record of disinterested public service. Thus it seems
that Thailand in the 1990s will remain democratic but that the King and the
army will continue to play a role which would be described in a Western democracy as that of 'checks and balances' on the excesses of elected politicians.

The question of political corruption is one which cannot be avoided in
South East Asia since it is almost endemic to the culture and may have started
in the perfectly innocent and traditional Asian custom of subjects giving their
rulers gifts and rulers granting them favours in return for their presents. Such
a role has now been taken on by the elected politicians in Japan, in Indonesia,
Malaysia and Thailand. The clear ethical judgement which would be made
about Western politicians taking such bribes or gifts cannot be made with the
same confidence in the traditional Asian culture. Nevertheless, the increased
attention of the Asian press on this topic has forced the resignations of several
Japanese cabinet ministers. If the corruption is taken to excess, as it clearly was
in the case of Marcos in the Philippines, it may provide the moral justification
for a change of government, whether by violent or non-violent means. This
clearly was also the case with the Thai Prime Minister Chatichai when he was
removed from power in a bloodless coup in Bangkok in early 1991. It was
simply considered that he had carried the traditional practice too far.

Political risk then in Thailand needs to be seen in this cultural context.
Thailand has been given a higher rating for political stability because of the
existence of the monarchy first of all. King Bhumibol, who has been on the
throne since 1946, commands enormous personal respect and popular
reverence. It is impossible, therefore, for any government or military group to
gain power without his tacit approval. This factor mitigates much of the
instability which may be suggested by the record for the past sixty years of
attempted military coups. At the same time Thailand has differed from its
neighbours Burma and Vietnam in possessing a free and independent peasant
population which has, on the whole, enjoyed a higher standard of living than
their neighbours and, therefore, the communist movement has never made
much headway among the rural people. On the other hand again, Thailand's
extraordinary economic growth in the 1980s (averaging 10 per cent per
annum) has put great strains not only on the urban environment because of
traffic jams and pollution, but also on the social and family system. Many rural
families have been forced to send their teenage children to the cities to find
employment. The contrast of living standards between Bangkok and the north
east provinces (an estimated per capita income would be perhaps US $2500
per annum for the former and less than US $500 per annum for the latter)
must eventually create social tensions and potential unrest. The *laissez-faire*
policy of the Bangkok government has thus far worked extremely well
although the lack of planning, in terms of the proliferation of factories around
the capital, leaves something to be desired.

Perhaps one indication of the political trend in Thailand's future is the popularity of the new and austere Buddhist Governor of Bangkok metropolitan area, Chamlong, who has publicly denounced the government for its corruption and lives rather in the style of a monk. The popular response to unbridled economic growth and materialism may well be a return to traditional Buddhist values. In any case, the fact that Thailand is a majority Buddhist country may do much to explain the non-violent changes of power and exchanges of politically different views which characterizes its public life. So, along with the monarchy we must count Buddhism as a major factor of political stability. The army is the third element which can be considered, on balance, to be a positive factor. During the 1970s when it seemed more than probable that Thailand would bear out the Pentagon 'dominoe theory' by which each country in succession – China in 1949, North Vietnam in 1954, South Vietnam in 1975, Laos, Cambodia in 1975–7 . . . Thailand, Malaysia, Singapore – would fall to the irresistible southward movement of the communist militias. But Thailand was the point at which communism stumbled and fell back. Much of this has to do with the professionalism of the army and the basic resistance of the people to a foreign ideology. As Siam had resisted British and French colonial pressure in the nineteenth century, so Thailand in the twentieth century resisted the Marxist Leninist dictatorship which engulfed its once prosperous neighbour, Vietnam. An even more striking contrast can be made with Burma which, when it gained independence from Britain in 1948, was a much more prosperous and successful country than Thailand, with a British-developed infrastructure and civil service and large natural resources in petroleum and precious minerals. The contrast in 1990 could not be greater and it is said that, when the Foreign Minister of Burma visited Bangkok recently, he wept when he realized how far his country had fallen behind.

So a further element in cementing the freedom, stability and independence of Thailand today, as Siam a century ago, is in this clear and well-publicized contrast with its neighbours. Thailand is, finally, the most open country to foreigners and receives almost 5 million tourists a year. The self-confidence and strong sense of cultural identity of the Thai people is in no way diminished by the superlative standards of service which characterize their hotels, tourist resorts and airlines. Any independent observer or visitor to Thailand can, therefore, assess the real nature of the underlying social stability of the country which supports the high degree of political stability predicted for the country.

ECONOMIC RISK

Thailand's economy has been the fastest growing in the world for the past three years. The take-off really began in 1986–7 with the flood of new foreign investment into the country, largely from Japan and Taiwan. The rapid appreciation of the Japanese yen against the dollar in 1985–6 forced many Japanese manufacturers to consider moving some of the low technology, low labour cost activities, such as textiles, consumer electronics and footwear, offshore. Thailand was a natural destination for Japan's industrialists, made easier by the low degree of red tape and bureaucratic delays. Hence we can see from the figures published by the Board of Investment between 1985 and 1991 that the rising tide of foreign capital was a major cause of Thailand's economic boom. GNP growth reached over 12 per cent in 1988 and 1989 and it seems likely that in the 1990s Thailand can sustain a medium-term growth of nearly 7 per cent annually in real terms.

There has been a large shift away from agriculture towards manufacturing. As recently as 1980, 50 per cent of Thailand's exports consisted of rice and tapioca and other agricultural products. By 1990, 75 per cent of the total volume of exports were manufactured goods, mainly from the newly established assembly plants in Bangkok and the south. This has resulted in large changes in employment and moves of populations. Nevertheless, the profound change in the structure of Thailand's economy has been well absorbed and sets the stage for a move into higher value added products in the years up to 2000.

INFLATION RISK

It is surprising, considering the very high rate of economic growth that the economy has experienced, that prices, as measured by the consumer price index, have been kept under control. The last serious bout of inflation in Thailand occurred during the two oil crises, first in 1973–4 when the CPI touched 24 per cent and then again in 1980–1 when there was a resurgence of inflation to nearly 20 per cent. In the later 1980s, and thanks largely to a more stable oil price, inflation has been held in single digits and has not exceeded 6 per cent. Nevertheless, the boom of the past three years, particularly in Bangkok, has led to a rapid escalation of real estate values and rents. It is likely that the slowdown in the economy in 1991 will result in a lower inflation rate and, therefore, it is expected that Thailand's inflation will be held at 5 per cent or below in the next few years.

EXCHANGE RATE RISK

Once again the record is one of extraordinary stability. The Thai baht has been carefully managed by the Bank of Thailand against a basket of currencies which is thought to be around 80 per cent dollars and 20 per cent yen. When measured against the US dollar it has resulted in a very small annual variation of less than 3 or 4 per cent. In fact, during the last six years there has been virtually no change in the value of the baht compared with the dollar. Clearly, the weaker dollar of the 1985–90 period has favoured Thailand's exports. (The same effect is observable with the Hong Kong dollar which is also pegged to the American unit.) Therefore, it is expected that Thailand's currency will remain extremely stable in dollar terms in the future.

FOREIGN TRADE RISK

Considering the rapid growth of exports in recent years it is, nevertheless, a fact that Thailand has consistently run a small trade deficit which is normally covered by the substantial inflow of earnings from tourism on the current account. Thus Thailand's overall financial position remains healthy on a year-to-year basis although its imports have remained rather strong during this period of high economic growth. Being a very open economy (and indeed the Bank of Thailand removed all foreign exchange controls in late 1990) there are no restrictions on purchases of foreign goods and the economy relies on a policy of providing competitive home made products (sometimes without regard to international copyright) to keep its trade in balance.

MALAYSIA

Table 5.7 gives details of the overall economic performance of Malaysia from 1970 to 1990.

POLITICAL RISK

The central dilemma in assessing Malaysia's political risk is the perennial question of relations between the Malay and Chinese communities representing as they do about 60 per cent and 30 per cent of the population respectively. Since the 1969 anti-Chinese riots in Kuala Lumpur the country has been unruffled by any serious inter-racial violence and during this period a great deal has been accomplished in transforming the economy and in transferring the wealth of the country from foreign and Chinese hands into the hands of the *bumiputra* (or the sons of the soil), which is the dominant Malay majority. The success of this New Economic Policy is unquestioned and has given a great deal of legitimacy to the continued run of the United Malay National Organisation (UMNO) under its successive prime ministers and most recently under Dr. Mahathir Mohammed who has now held power for almost a decade. This economic success has also done much to defuse the threat from the Islamic fundamentalists who have tended to get co-opted into the ruling party. The Chinese community has also done well in economic terms although the political disunity in the Malay Chinese Association (MCA) has left them somewhat leaderless in the political sphere.

Politics in Malaysia continues to be a question to revolve around the leading

Table 5.7. Economic profile of Malaysia, 1970–90

	Exchange rate ag. US $	GNP/ GDP growth (%)	CPI	Trade surplus/ (deficit) (US $mn)	P/E	Total turnover (US $mn)	Market year-end closing	Market capital (US $bn)
1970	–		–	349				
1971	–		–	225				
1972	2.187 0		3.23	129				
1973	2.452 0		10.52	652				
1974	2.312 8		17.51	224				
1975	2.588 3		4.56	256				
1976	2.535 0		2.64	1 464				
1977	2.365 5		4.78	1 519				
1978	2.206 0		4.86	1 593				
1979	2.189 0		3.66	3 157		749.7		
1980	2.222 4		6.67	2 406	26.1	519.9		
1981	2.242 3		9.70	(105)	25.2	3 594.3		
1982	2.321 3		5.84	(753)	24.9	1 401.2		
1983	2.338 3	6.3	3.71	432	32.0	3 393.2		22.79
1984	2.425 0	7.6	3.91	2 981	21.0	2 356.2		19.59
1985	2.426 5	−1.1	0.35	3 577	18.0	2 542.6		16.44
1986	2.603 0	1.2	0.74	3 245	40.1	1 299.0	252.26	14.98
1987	2.492 8	5.4	0.88	5 835	26.8	4 042.6	261.19	18.49
1988	2.175 3	8.9	1.96	5 546	36.0	3 107.8	357.38	29.05
1989	2.703 3	8.8	2.82	3 899	29.9	6 856.6	562.28	39.73
1990	2.698 0	10.0	5.00	179	20.8	10 861.1	501.00	48.81

personalities such as Mahathir. It should also be noted, however, that Malaysia shares one characteristic with Thailand, which is a strong monarchical system. In Malaysia's case it is less visible because the kingship is shared on a five-year revolving basis among the sultans of the various states of the federation. The present *Yang di-Pertnan, Agong,* or king, is the former Sultan of Selangor and a highly respected man who has also served the Chief Justice of Malaysia. This clear distinction of the British model between the head of state, or monarch, and the prime minister, or political leader, is important to Malaysia's overall stability.

The geographical divide between peninsular Malaysia and East Malaysia, consisting of the states of Sabah and Sarawak, also underlines the need for a great deal of political decentralization. Sabah and Sarawak have very different histories from the other Malaysian states and can be examined for their political make-up on a separate basis including the question of the Christian minority in Sabah. Overall, however, one must judge that Malaysia's economic success has led to a far greater degree of political stability than was expected following independence in 1963.

An historian must take a more dispassionate long-term outlook and say that the ethnic make-up of Malaysia could again lead to strains in the future particularly if economic growth should falter. In addition, Malaysia has only 18 million people and has a shortage of skilled labour. It is estimated that between 1 and 2 million Indonesians are presently working illegally in the country, mainly on the plantations. This immigrant labour population could also lead to friction in the future.

Malaysia's relations with its neighbours on the whole are excellent and, in particular, the relationship with Singapore, which remains the largest investor in the country, is a key one. The Singapore government is obviously enthusiastic to diversify its industrial base across the causeway into Johore and further north into peninsular Malaysia. This is good news for Malaysia's economic and political stability.

ECONOMIC RISK

Malaysia, along with Singapore, experienced a sharp recession in 1985–6 owing to an excessively tight monetary policy in both countries. Since 1987 Malaysia has, however, returned to the path of high growth and low inflation, recording a real GNP growth in excess of 8 per cent in the past three years with inflation averaging between 2 and 3 per cent. Nevertheless, over a twenty year period Malaysia ranks behind Singapore, Thailand and Hong Kong, although ahead of Indonesia in past overall economic growth. The change in the past three years has also been accompanied by an accelerated shift into manufacturing and away from the old dependence on the plantation sector. This manufacturing growth has been led by investment from Japan and Taiwan and notable national projects such as the Proton car. Malaysia is attempting to move up market into the new product areas such as electronics, car assembly and consumer goods. It is likely to be successful in doing so owing to its literate and trainable workforce. Therefore, one can be fairly confident that Malaysia's economic record will continue to be bright.

EXCHANGE RATE RISK

The exchange rate of the Malaysian ringgit has been closely tied to that of the Singapore dollar which itself has been very stable if not strong against other world currencies especially the US dollar. Therefore, the ringgit has had a very stable record against the dollar and is likely to maintain this stability. Malaysia's foreign trade has generally been in surplus, recording a positive balance of between US $4–5 billion each year. In 1990 this figure fell sharply partly owing to fall-off in Malaysia's energy exports. As manufactured goods assume a larger importance in the composition of exports compared with crude oil, rubber and palm oil, Malaysia's trade position should gradually become steadier. For an investor Malaysia remains attractive although vulnerable to external shocks either in terms of commodity prices or in a fall in export demand in its principal markets. The infrastructure, high literacy rate and relative political stability in recent years are all bonus points for the country's overall image.

SINGAPORE

Table 5.8 gives details of the overall economic performance of Singapore from 1970 to 1990.

Table 5.8. Economic profile of Singapore, 1970–90

	Exchange rate ag. US $	GNP/ GDP growth (%)	CPI	Trade surplus/ (deficit) (US $mn)	P/E	Total turnover (US $mn)	Market year-end closing	Market capital (US $bn)
1970	–	13.7	–				139.06	
1971	–	12.5	–				197.69	
1972	2.820 0	13.4	3.1				432.73	
1973	2.486 1	11.5	18.4				265.57	
1974	2.312 0	6.3	23.0				150.82	
1975	2.489 5	4.1	2.7				236.76	
1976	2.455 5	7.5	−1.9				254.51	
1977	2.338 5	7.8	3.2				264.24	
1978	2.163 5	8.6	4.8				349.16	
1979	2.159 0	9.3	4.0		17.9	1 070.6	435.41	
1980	2.093 5	9.7	8.6		22.6	3 737.6	660.82	
1981	2.047 8	9.6	8.2		22.1	6 578.8	780.78	
1982	2.108 5	6.9	4.0		18.8	2 455.2	732.32	
1983	2.127 0	8.2	1.2	(6 276.0)	27.5	5 551.1	1 002.03	12.22
1984	2.178 0	8.3	2.6	(4 496.8)	18.9	3 770.1	812.61	9.92
1985	2.105 0	−1.6	0.5	(3 629.0)	16.6	3 002.0	620.04	11.07
1986	2.175 0	1.8	−1.4	(3 016.1)	35.2	3 678.4	891.30	16.60
1987	1.998 5	8.8	0.5	(4 077.6)	21.3	11 247.5	823.58	17.86
1988	1.946 2	11.1	1.5	(4 714.8)	20.9	6 585.7	1 038.62	24.00
1989	1.894 4	9.2	2.4	(5 145.7)	19.0	20 666.12	1 481.33	35.95
1990	1.745 5	8.3	3.2	(8 364.4)	15.3	20 963.6	1 154.48	34.26

Note: Market capital figures for Singapore for incorporated companies only.

POLITICAL RISK

'The silent success', in the words of a Singapore government minister, of this region is based on a high literacy rate and a well-educated and trainable workforce (Koh Beng Seng, Deputy Managing Director – Monetary Authority of Singapore, conversation with author). The investment in human capital has proven to be more important to a lasting economic growth success story than the availability of finance or technology. The demise of communism is also promoting greater confidence and political stability in the Association of South East Asian Nations (ASEAN) region, of which Singapore is the *de facto* financial centre.

Essentially Singapore's aim in the 1990s will be to emulate what Hong Kong has done in Guangdong Province and the hinterland of southern China. But in Singapore's case its export of jobs and lower value added industries will be mainly to neighbouring Malaysia and, to a lesser extent, to Indonesia. 'Malaysia is not essentially a labour surplus country,' (Koh Beng Seng as above). The plantations in the southern part of the Malaysian peninsular depend almost entirely on the large annual in-take of illegal workers from Indonesia. With 100 million people in Java alone, Indonesia needs to provide employment for 2–3 million a year. Thus mobility of labour within ASEAN is as important, if not more so, than mobility of capital.

Singapore is aiming its investment at Johore in Malaysia and Batam Island in Indonesia. This is the so-called growth triangle. There is a political aspect to this. Singapore is a small Chinese island surrounded by a sea of Muslims. It needs to ensure political stability among its neighbours. One of the best ways of doing this (as Hong Kong has found in southern China) is to invest and create jobs and raise per capita incomes from their present low level.

The other aspect of political risk when considering Singapore is, of course, the handover of political power from one generation to another (a common theme throughout the Asian countries). Although Lee Kwan Yew stepped down as Prime Minister in 1990, he continues to wield a large influence and power behind the scenes, particularly in his role as General Secretary of the People's Action Party (PAP). He has dominated the PAP as he has dominated Singapore for the past thirty years. Nowhere in the world could it be truer to say that the state is the creation of one man, thus his succession poses a very real problem. His son, Lee Hsien Loong, often known as BG or Brigadier General, is just 40 years old and may not take up the post of Prime Minister for three to five years. In any case, the question of dynastic succession in a parliamentary democracy, even within a limited Confucian Chinese democracy, is, to say the least, a questionable one. Many of the elder Lee's policies, such as imposing the Mandarin Chinese language on the Singapore educational system, have aroused fierce opposition among the older, anti-communist generation of Singapore Chinese. Some of them have emigrated to Australia and elsewhere as a result. The tight control of the media and the suppression of all political opposition or criticism of the government, the PAP or the Prime Minister himself, has also aroused criticism both at home and internationally.

But, on balance, nobody can objectively doubt the enormous success of Lee Kwan Yew's achievement in creating modern Singapore. It is clean, efficient and notably lacking in corruption compared to other Asian cities. The Central Provident Fund, which takes 35 per cent of every person's income as a compulsory savings scheme, has built up an enormous reservoir of capital for future use in Singapore. Notable public works such as Changi Airport or the transport system have been the result. Long-term planning has not been as successful anywhere else, with the possible exception of Japan. The paternalistic attitude of the Singapore government towards its citizens is unlikely to change in the immediate future especially since the younger generation of Singaporeans have been thoroughly versed in the disciplined Confucian thinking and authoritarianism which characterizes the school system as well as government. Singapore also has a well run and modern citizens' army based, like the Swiss model, on an annual call-up of every able-bodied man aged between 18 and 50. The city state is thus well equipped to defend itself against any aggressor. Singapore will also benefit from the inflow of human and financial capital from Hong Kong as 1997 approaches. In this sense it does not need to change but merely to retain its present stability and attractive lifestyle in order to continue to prosper. Thus, the conclusion to be drawn is that Singapore scores an equally high rating in terms of very low political risk and a high degree of stability as Japan.

ECONOMIC RISK

The Singapore economy has been characterized by the highest degree of government involvement and intervention outside of the socialist world. Nevertheless, the growth rate has been quite impressive, averaging around 7–8 per cent, except during the 1985–6 recession, and even more impressive has been the tight control of inflation which, along with that of Japan, has remained extremely low at below 3 per cent for the past decade. The economic stability of Singapore, therefore, scores high on a comparative basis although being a small island state it is very sensitive to developments in its two main neighbours, Indonesia and Malaysia, with their large commodity-based economies. Singapore's position is somewhat analogous to that of Switzerland, placed between France and Germany. But given that Singapore has only 2.3 million people, the service sector and particularly the financial sector are inevitably more important relative to Switzerland and the industrial sector is smaller. Thus, Singapore runs a regular trade deficit of around US $5 billion per annum which is easily covered by its current account surplus on invisibles. Singapore's foreign reserves held by the Monetary Authority of Singapore (MAS) and the Government Investment Corporation of Singapore (GICS) are estimated to be in excess of US $50 billion which would give this tiny Asian city state the third highest foreign exchange reserves after Japan and Taiwan.

Thus, the overall management of 'Singapore Inc.' is extremely conservative with a very high degree of self-reliance, a high savings rate and an ample cushion for unexpected global events. This financial conservatism has been reflected in the strong performance of the Singapore dollar which has advanced steadily against the US dollar during the past five years with an average appreciation of 5 per cent per annum. It is reasonable to expect these trends – high economic growth, high savings rate, low inflation and steady currency appreciation – to continue during the 1990s. The financial figures, therefore, confirm the political analysis we have made of Singapore as having a very low risk in absolute terms.

INDONESIA

Table 5.9 gives details of the overall economic performance of Indonesia from 1970 to 1990.

Table 5.9. Economic profile of Indonesia, 1970–90

	Exchange rate ag. US $	GNP/ GDP growth (%)	CPI	Trade surplus/ (deficit) (US $mn)	P/E	Total turnover (US $mn)	Market year-end closing	Market capital (US $bn)
1970	–							
1971	–		–					
1972	415		6.5					
1973	415		31.1					
1974	415		41.1					
1975	415		19.1					
1976	415		19.9					
1977	415		11.1					
1978	625		8.2					
1979	627		20.7					
1980	627		18.5					
1981	644		12.4					
1982	693		9.5				95.00	
1983	994	4.2	11.8				80.37	
1984	1 074	6.7	10.5			1.94	63.53	0.08
1985	1 125	2.5	4.7			2.79	66.53	0.08
1986	1 641	4.0	5.8	4 100		1.08	69.69	0.06
1987	1 650	3.6	9.0	4 600		3.07	82.58	0.07
1988	1 731	5.6	7.4	4 900	41.2	16.90	305.12	0.26
1989	1 797	7.4	6.0	5 800	24.7	524.75	399.69	2.42
1990	1 901	7.1	9.6	3 986	19.9	4 943.30	417.79	3.87

POLITICAL RISK

It can at least be argued that Indonesia has had fewer changes in its political system than its Asian neighbours. In fact, there have been only two rulers of

Indonesia since independence was gained from the Dutch in 1948 – Sukarno and Suharto. But equally it should not be forgotten that the two major turning points in the country's modern history – independence and the 1965 revolution – so vividly depicted in the film *The Year of Living Dangerously* – were unusually violent episodes in the life of any country. The stability which Indonesia has enjoyed during the past twenty-five years under Suharto should, therefore, be placed against this background.

In many ways the same three pillars of stability which we have analyzed in Thailand – the army, the king and the national religion – are present in Indonesia except that the President, Suharto, stands in the place of the monarchy and the national religion is Islam rather than Buddhism. The question of monarchical or presidential succession remains perhaps the major political risk confronted by the foreign investor as so many aspects of the business life of the country relate directly to Suharto or his immediate family. The role of the army in Indonesia is a great deal more clear cut and predictable than in either Thailand or in the Philippines. In effect, there have been no attempted military coups since 1966. The army remains wholly in support of Suharto. It has been suggested, in fact, that anyone who might be considered as a candidate to succeed Suharto must be Javanese and must be a general.

The role of Islam in the national life of Indonesia is a more complex subject. The Mohammedan religion first reached the shores of western Sumatra through the coming of the Arab traders around 1400. The western-most state of Aceh has remained a stronghold of Islamic fundamentalist belief ever since. Sumatra in general has remained restive and unwilling to bend to the yoke of a tight central control from Java. In fact, this is also true of many other island provinces of the huge Indonesian archipelago which will have, by the year 2000, a population of over 200 million. Following the 1958 uprising in Sumatra and Celebes (or Sulawesi) the Javanese policy was to plant more settlers in these outlying islands from Java (where 80 per cent of the population lives). Political and religious factors, therefore, cannot be disentangled in the future horoscope of Indonesian political life.

Fundamentalism is on the rise, as also in Malaysia, and politicians with fundamentalist Islamic beliefs and supporters are likely to take a more active role. However, the situation cannot be compared with Iran or Saudi Arabia. In neither Indonesia nor Malaysia has Islam taken over all aspects of every day life with its rules about the role of women or the consumption of alcohol or the exaction of interest or usury on capital. In all these respects Indonesian life is relatively 'modern'. There is a more easy-going Asian approach to matters of religious belief.

However, the social question, which we cannot ignore, concerns the role of the minority and non-Muslim peoples in Indonesia, in particular the Chinese community in Java. Although the total Chinese population is less than 5 million, or around 3 per cent of the total, 80 per cent of the commerce and much of the capital wealth remains in the hands of this small but tight-knit Chinese community. In 1966 there were violent anti-Chinese riots and killings in Jakarta, Surabaya and other Javanese cities. Many thousands of Chinese fled to Hong Kong and to China but this is a spectre which has been banished from the life of the nation since Suharto came to power. He is well known to have close links with the leading members of the Chinese business community such as Liem Sioe Long.

The role of Chinese businesspeople in Indonesia has been brought into much greater focus by the explosion of the Jakarta stockmarket in the past two years since 1988. Much of the wealth which was rumoured to exist in the hands of the great Chinese families such as Liem, Soeradjaya, Hui the palm oil king, and Riady, is now visibly calculated on a daily basis in the large listed capitalization of the Indonesian-Chinese industrial groups such as Indo-Cement and Astra. There is, of course, a two-way flow of capital involved in this process of the rapid evolution of the capital market in Jakarta, by which up to US $5 billion of foreign capital has entered the country in the form of equity investment, largely from foreign fund managers, and a substantial amount of Chinese capital has been able to leave the country in the opposite direction.

Nobody doubts the enormous economic potential of Indonesia, its vast natural resources and its large labour force being two principal attractions. However, the main element of political risk is the possibility of a further violent episode in the political life of the country when the next transfer of power occurs at the top.

ECONOMIC RISK

Indonesia began the 1980s principally as an oil exporter. During the 1970s it had had a high rate of inflation but also a very rapid economic growth on the back of the oil boom. The fall in oil prices in the early 1980s, which became precipitate in the spring of 1986, therefore, forced the technocrats at the Ministry of Finance in Jakarta to review thoroughly their priorities. Reducing inflation, diversifying the economy away from oil and maintaining a stable growth in the economy to provide as full employment as possible for the large young population, were selected as the main objectives. It is remarkable to see the extent to which these aims have been achieved during 1985–90. Inflation has been brought from 20 per cent, at the beginning of the decade, to around 6 per cent in 1989–90. Economic growth, having fallen to 2.5 per cent in 1985 regained the level of 7.5 per cent by 1990. The rupiah, which had undergone a 30 per cent once-and-for-all evaluation in the autumn of 1985, had stabilized on a 'crawling peg' system with an annual devaluation of around 5 per cent. The trade surplus continued at a healthy US $4–5 billion annually and the inflow of foreign capital more than offset Indonesia's foreign debt position. Therefore, it is possible to conclude that the good macroeconomic

management, which was achieved by the small group of technocrats employed
by Suharto to direct the economy, had been very successful in reducing the
economic risk of the country. The future path of the Indonesian economy will,
therefore, depend as much on the development of low wage manufacturing
and the inflow of Japanese capital, on the liberalization of the banking system
and the capital market, as on the price of basic commodities. This gives a
much greater degree of stability to the Indonesian economy as a whole.

THE PHILIPPINES

Table 5.10 gives details of the overall economic performance of the
Philippines from 1970 to 1990.

Table 5.10. Economic profile of the Philippines, 1970–90

	Exchange rate ag. US $	GNP/ GDP growth (%)	CPI	Trade surplus/ (deficit) (US $mn)	P/E	Total turnover (US $mn)	Market year-end closing	Market capital (US $bn)
1970	–		–					
1971	–		–					
1972	6.781		8.4					
1973	6.730		16.6					
1974	7.065		34.5					
1975	7.498		7.0					
1976	7.428		9.2					
1977	7.370		9.9					
1978	7.375		7.4					
1979	7.415		17.5					
1980	7.600		18.4					
1981	8.200		13.2					
1982	9.171		10.2					
1983	14.002		10.0					
1984	19.760	−6.8	50.3	(679)	5.8	156.0	100.29	0.83
1985	19.032	−3.8	23.1	(482)	4.9	52.8	131.19	0.67
1986	20.530	2.0	0.8	(202)	3.8	408.0	424.81	2.02
1987	20.800	5.7	3.8	(1 017)	7.9	921.6	642.72	2.97
1988	21.350	6.7	8.8	(1 085)	19.6	456.0	841.65	4.20
1989	22.440	5.7	10.6	(2 598)	16.8	2 116.8	1 145.45	11.82
1990	28.000	3.1	14.2	(4 010)	13.8	1 411.2	651.78	5.73

POLITICAL RISK

The Philippines is a special case in Asia. Culturally and politically it has a very
distinct national personality. The Roman Catholic Church plays a leading role

in its national life, not least in recent political changes. The fact that the Philippines was the only American colony in Asia also gave it a very different tradition from Indonesia or Malaysia, which had similar languages but very different cultural traditions. The Spanish occupation of the previous four hundred years also left some deeper traces than the Dutch did in Indonesia. (Filipino history has been wryly described as '400 years in a Spanish convent and 50 years in Hollywood' by General MacArthur.)

When speaking of political risk, however, the real problem in the Philippines has been the lack of legitimacy which has plagued successive governments and has led to the constant pendulum between dictatorship and weak democratic governments. Filipinos also tend to look to their presidents to be supermen and when they turn out, in fact, not to live up to this star-billing there is an enormous sense of popular disappointment.

One key personality is, of course, General MacArthur. The US tutelage has left a lasting imprint and the question of the US bases is still a very divisive issue in Philippine national opinion. The charismatic leadership of Magsaysay in the 1950s also left a vivid example to his successors. The attempts, in the 1960s, to solve the enormous economic problems of the Philippines, especially the rural poverty and the rapid growth of population, were not successful when pursued in a socialist direction. Marcos arrived in power in 1965 and inherited a country which still had higher living standards than most other Asian countries such as Hong Kong, Korea, Taiwan and Singapore. Therefore, judgement on his twenty year rule must be very negative as a result, if only judged as an economic failure.

The question most investors, therefore, raise is whether the Philippines is capable of responsible government and economic planning which would give it a GNP growth rate approaching that of its Asian tiger neighbours. Many observers dismiss this prospect out of hand citing the endemic problems of corruption, political in-fighting and the lack of the Confucian work ethic present in North Asia. However, there is no doubt that the Philippines possesses enormous natural advantages and it would be wrong to generalize about the whole archipelago of 7,000 islands from the political life of Manila alone. The island of Cebu, for example, has seen a successful economic transformation in the past twenty years. Manufacturing investment has grown and has begun to replace agriculture as a principal source of employment. The Philippines has a very high rate of literacy and the work ethic cannot be doubted by anyone who has employed Filipino domestic workers overseas. Their earnings are an important source of remittance back to the Philippines each year. The Filipino population in the United States is now the largest Asian ethnic group in that country approaching 2 million, mainly in California. Both natural resources, therefore, and an intelligent, hardworking population favour the country.

Unfortunately, the political system has never been able to maintain the long-term stability for its promise to be fulfilled. The last five years, during which Corazon Aquino has restored democratic procedures to Philippine political life, have also been disappointing in that many of the features of Washington political life have been reproduced in Manila – continuous discord between Congress, Senate and the President, making important national decisions extremely difficult to reach. On top of that, of course, there have been the continuing attempts by the military to unseat the elected government – there have been eight attempted *coup d'etats* since Aquino came to power. Although all of these have failed they have, nevertheless, done much to undermine the confidence of international investors in the political stability of the country. In particular, the failed attempt of December 1989 led to a slump in the economy and the stockmarket and scared away much needed foreign capital.

There are signs in 1991 that Japanese and Taiwanese investors and banks are coming back to the Philippines. The signing of a final accord with the United States on the future of the two major bases at Clark and Subic Bay is an important pointer to the future. The coming presidential elections in May 1992 will finally settle the question of whether the Philippines can assure a smooth continuation in its elected democratic leadership. Nevertheless, it can only be concluded that democracy is a fragile plant in the Philippines which may be snuffed out in the future as it has been in the past. There is continued rivalry for political and business influence among a small group of leading Filipino families. The press, although perhaps the freest in Asia, is considered to be irresponsible and corrupt and does much to undermine the legitimacy of the ruling government. Political risk, therefore, is judged to be higher here than in other Asian countries.

ECONOMIC RISK

In the previous paragraphs the economic impact of the failed *coup d'etat* of 1989 was outlined. The GNP growth, which had been running at 6 per cent average for the previous three years, fell to only 3 per cent in 1990 and inflation rose to 14 per cent. The peso was rather weak, falling from 20 to 28 to the US dollar, and the trade deficit doubled to nearly US $4 billion. The stockmarket tumbled by over 50 per cent, from a high of 1145 to less than 600, and the overall value of listed Philippine shares fell from US $12 billion to less than US $6 billion. Such is the real economic risk for investors of this fragile political system. Nevertheless, the recovery of confidence in early 1991 is testament to the long-term value that investors see in the country. Even if relative to its Asian neighbours the Philippines continues to have economic problems (and notably its high foreign debt), it will benefit from regional trends and it will present, from time to time, very interesting buying opportunities. The educated and literate labour force is a major resource of wages and relatively low taxes.

INFLATION RISK

At the worst point of the last years of the Marcos regime inflation in the Philippines reached 50 per cent, the highest recorded in Asia during the past decade. With the strong support of the central bank under Governor Jobo Fernandez, the money supply was reined in, the peso was stablized and inflation came down to single digits between 1986 and 1988. It has recently risen again to nearly 15 per cent in 1990 and clearly presents a serious risk for investment managers. Nevertheless, the tight monetary policy has been maintained and interest rates have been as high as 35 per cent to control the supply of credit. Therefore, with good macroeconomic management the inflation problems in the Philippines can be contained.

EXCHANGE RATE RISK

The same rule can be applied to the value of the peso which has had a poor long-term record and, despite the efforts of a strong and independent central bank, has again slid in value against the dollar in the past two years. With the benefit of strict International Monetary Fund (IMF) prescriptions it is hoped that the Philippines will now be able to reschedule its foreign debt particularly with the help of the Japanese banks, stabilize the currency and maintain a reasonable growth in its export trade.

6

EMERGING ASIAN CAPITAL MARKETS

INTRODUCTION TO STOCKMARKETS

The idea of a stockmarket is a relatively modern one having started in London in the early eighteenth century and in New York in 1792. The first stockmarket in Asia was set up by the British in Bombay in 1887 but the concept developed much later in the countries outside the British Empire. There was, for example, no stockmarket in either French Indochina or in the Dutch East Indies. Under American influence the Manila stock exchange was established in 1927. Elsewhere it was really only in the post-war period that capital markets in Asia began to be established. Japan, of course, has had over a century of economic transformation and did have an active government bond market in the late nineteenth century. It was not until the 1960s that Taiwan, Korea or Thailand created their own stock exchanges and not until the 1980s that they began to be noticed by international investors.

It is important to emphasize, therefore, that this is a very recent social phenomenon and that the traditions and regulations of these stockmarkets are also very new. The cultural aspect of the stockmarket is not frequently emphasized but it is perhaps worth examining more closely. In the United Kingdom and the United States the idea of a joint stock company with a large number of shareholders goes back more than 250 years: the idea being that it is written in common law that shareholders will have equal voting rights and receive dividends from the company. The origin of a listed public company is more likely to be that of an initial flotation for public subscription than of an old established family company coming to the market to sell the owner's shares and create a public ownership.

The recent phenomenon of denationalization or privatization of large state-owned companies has also spread share ownership more widely than ever before. However, although the attitude of governments towards stockmarkets has undergone a significant change during the 1980s, it also reflects historical and social traditions of the market and in Asia often takes account of the fact that cabinet ministers and officials themselves will be buyers in the market. By contrast, in the older established Western markets the stock exchange grew up quite independently as a self-governing body of individual jobbers, traders and stockbrokers without too much government legislation. This was typified by the old London tradition of 'my word is my bond' which implied that little additional securities legislation or investor protection would be necessary than the social or peer pressure to keep one's word.

Very different is the world of the 1980s, both in London and in Asia. But it is still true to say that the concept of insider trading is not widely understood in the new financial centres such as Bangkok, Jakarta, Manila or Seoul, and certainly not subject to the same severe penalties as it would be in New York, London or even Hong Kong today. The new stockmarkets in Asia which have developed in the last twenty years have been, from the beginning, much more directed and encouraged by enlightened and pro-business governments with a view to channelling domestic savings into enterprises. This is particularly true of the Japanese model which has served as an inspiration for many other Asian stock exchanges. Clearly, the extraordinary financial wealth which was created in Tokyo and Osaka in the past twenty years reflected the great economic success of Japan's exporters, but it is also true to say that it would not have grown as successfully as it did over such a long period of time (see Figure 6.1) if it had not been for careful, long-term planning and institutional support. This involved the Ministry of Finance, the big banks, the four major brokerage houses and many of the large listed companies themselves, especially those of the trading houses or *zaibatsu* groups. These formed the core of the market listings, were the 'blue chips' of the Tokyo index and, through their extensive cross-holdings with one another, formed a very efficient support system for share prices across the board in times of crisis or recession. The Tokyo market has often been studied by Western analysts and especially after the October 1987 crash, which illustrated the very different cultural character of Tokyo compared with New York and other Western markets. Ultimately, however, the Tokyo market proved to be no more immune to the fundamental value measurements than any other market, in particular to the rising cost of money, reflected in higher Japanese interest rates, or to the weakening of real estate values, which had been a principal justification for the high values of share prices.

Korea and Taiwan were both former Japanese colonies with a strong Japanese cultural influence and their capital markets reflected much of the Japanese model. In Korea the *chaebol* performed much the same role as had the *zaibatsu* in Japan. Hyundai, Samsung, Daewoo and Lucky formed the core of the stockmarket as they did of the Korean economy, in much the same way as Mitsui, Mitsubishi, Yasuda and Fuji groups had represented the core of the Japanese market and economy. The close relationship between the banks and the trading and manufacturing houses both assisted and, to some extent,

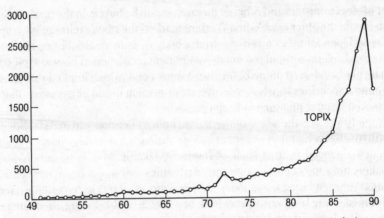

Figure 6.1. Performance of the Topix 1949–90 (Tokyo stock price index)

restrained the amount of capital raising that could be done on the stockmarket. But basically the close interlocking relationships of these large groups, between themselves and between business and government, lent a great deal of stability and support to these Asian stockmarkets in the early days of their development. Taiwan was certainly much more freewheeling in keeping with its largely unregulated economy. But the degree of regulation of Taiwan's stockmarket is surprisingly high, given its reputation as an Asian casino, where the capitalization of a Taiwanese bank, for example, has on occasions exceeded US $10 billion – rather more than Citibank is valued at in the New York market. Apart from the banks, however, the multiples of the Taiwanese stocks have not been excessive and the manufacturing shares have reflected the strong export performance which are a consistent feature of this Chinese island economy.

The 1980s saw an extraordinary spread of the idea of the stock exchange throughout Asia. This began with Japan and, by the latter part of the decade, Japan had astonished the world once again by having a larger stockmarket than America (aided, it is true, by the 50 per cent appreciation of the yen against the dollar). The number of investors, both domestic and foreign, in the Japanese market grew with the performance of the market, to include many Tokyo housewives and taxi drivers. But the most rapid growth was certainly in the newly established markets such as Bangkok, Seoul, Taipei and, latterly, Jakarta. The figures for Korea are extraordinary in that the number of investors multiplied by a factor of ten times during the decade and, according to the official statistics, accounted for almost 25 per cent of the total Korean population by 1990. (This, however, is thought to include many multiple name accounts.) In Bangkok, too, in the late 1980s some of the stockbroking houses opened offices in many small provincial towns in northern Thailand, enrolling farmers and shopkeepers as first-time investors.

The most extraordinary example of this social phenomenon may be observed in India where it was spearheaded by the Unit Trust of India (UTI), a very aggressive and entrepreneurial organization in Bombay. During the 1980s the assets under management of UTI grew twenty times to over US $7 billion and accounted for over fifty different types of unit trusts. The company employed 30,000 salespeople who often visited small Indian villages travelling on bicycles and selling unit trusts to peasants. The products they sold would include family growth trusts, which would be sold to grandparents as savings for their children and grandchildren and also to many Indian middle class couples to provide for their ageing parents. Almost in the spirit of the English Quakers, therefore, a charitable and family spirit was suggested in the sale of mutual funds. It is now estimated that there are more than 10 million unit holders and investors out of a total Indian middle class population of about 150 million and a total national population exceeding 850 million. This will give the reader some idea of the potential for further growth for the stockmarket phenomenon in what is generally perceived as being a very poor country. India, nevertheless, possesses an enormous pool of domestic savings and middle class wealth which may continue to be channelled into the growing stock exchange. There are now more than twenty stock exchanges spread throughout India with a capitalization of close to US $60 billion. The same phenomenon may be beginning in other countries as diverse as Pakistan, Bangladesh and Sri Lanka and may eventually be observed in some of the socialist nations.

The most remarkable example today is that of the Peoples Republic of China which, during the Maoist period, between 1949 and 1976, had perhaps gone further in the direction of total state control and state ownership than any other communist country. The beginnings of reform were made in 1978 with the decision of Deng Xiaoping to allow farmers to grow and sell their own produce rather than simply work on the collective or state-owned farms. This led directly to the tripling of peasant incomes especially in southern China during the 1980s, and to the dramatic growth in consumer spending on simple items such as bicycles, sewing machines, radios and eventually television sets which have transformed China in the past decade. This new-found peasant wealth eventually found its way into the cities and the economic reforms began to spread to small businesses, shops and light industries. China's first bond issue was in 1984 and the first share was issued in 1986 in Shanghai. From those small beginnings the market has developed steadily so that today there is a national Chinese bond market estimated to total more than US $50 billion in size. Small stock exchanges now exist in five different cities, the most notable being in Shanghai which has eight of the fifteen listed shares in China (in early 1991). There is little doubt in the mind of most foreign observers that this aspect of China's economic reforms will be taken much further in the 1990s and that, like India, it will be seen that in China there is a large and growing middle class whose savings have few attractive outlets. If a national share market is allowed to develop it will do so dramatically as a natural consequence of the tremendous economic growth which China has experienced in the 1980s.

This is a consistent theme of the sections in the following chapter on individual Asian countries. Capital market growth follows logically on economic growth and investors pay most attention to this fundamental tenet. Of course, along with economic growth, there must be currency stability and low inflation but, in whatever political system, the key elements are the growth of the economy, and the creation of wealth and savings, which are able to propel the high performance which has been typical of Asian stockmarkets in the 1980s.

ASIAN STOCKMARKETS

The out-performance of Asian share markets during the past ten years has been well documented but it is worth looking at the figures to compare them with the returns which investors have achieved in the US market and in European stockmarkets over the same length of time. Despite the recent fall in the Tokyo stockmarket, Japan has, over a longer period of time, performed phenomenally well. If we consider that in the year 1968 both the New York Dow Jones and the Nikkei Dow Jones were standing at an index level of 1000 (see Figure 6.2) and that as of May 1991 the Japanese index was trading at around 25,000 compared with a level of 3,000 in New York, it is possible to appreciate the compounded return which investors, who were prepared to take a long-term view of Asia, have been able to achieve.

The purpose of this book, however, is not to look so much at the past as at the future and it is very likely that in the 1990s and in the early years of the next century we shall continue to see an out-performance by Asian markets over those in the West for all the reasons that have been outlined in previous chapters. The focus of this out-performance, however, will no longer be Japan but the smaller Asian markets such as South Korea, Taiwan and Hong Kong (and possibly new markets in China), Thailand, Malaysia, Singapore and Indonesia. It is in these small, fast developing markets that there is still a 'catch up' effect of the capital market compared with the economy. It is also in these markets that savings rates continue to be extremely high compared with the West and will, therefore, provide a constant flow of new capital and liquidity to the local capital markets.

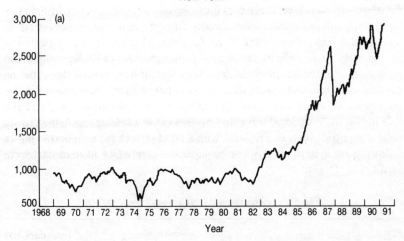

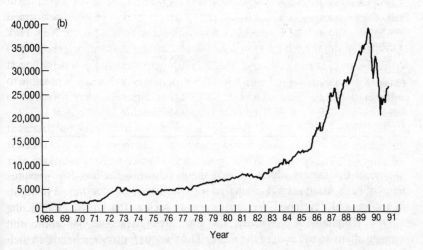

Figure 6.2. Comparison of the New York Dow Jones index and the Japan Nikkei Dow Jones index, 1 January 1968 to 30 May 1991, monthly: (a) New York Dow Jones industrials; (b) Japan Nikkei stock average (225). (*Source:* Datastream.)

Turning again to the fundamentals and looking at the comparative real GNP growth rates (see Table 6.1) it can be seen that the average in Asia has been 7 per cent real growth annually over the past twenty years compared with 3 per cent or less in Europe and North America. This trend can be expected to be maintained over the next decade. Although much will depend on the preservation of the international free trade system it is, nevertheless, true to say that inter-regional growth in Asian trade has become a major factor in the continuing superior performance of Asian countries. Japan will play a major role in this inter-regional trade and investment but the biggest beneficiaries will be countries such as Thailand, with a rapid growth in its exports to Japan following on a large investment by Japanese companies in manufacturing facilities in Thailand.

Table 6.1. Comparative real GNP growth rates, 1971–90

Country	High	Low	Average	Rank	Compounded growth over the period	Rank	1991F	Rank	Overall rating
South Korea	14.4	−3.0	8.7	2	428.0	2	8.7	1	1
Taiwan	14.0	1.2	8.9	1	448.3	1	6.4	6	2
Singapore	13.4	−1.6	8.1	4	367.0	3	7.2	3	3
Thailand	12.2	3.5	7.2	5	296.8	5	7.0	4	4
Hong Kong	17.1	−0.1	8.1	3	365.0	4	4.6	8	5
Malaysia	11.7	−1.1	7.0	7	281.9	7	8.4	2	6
China	13.5	−3.0	7.1	6	286.9	6	6.0	7	7
Indonesia	11.3	2.2	6.6	8	254.6	8	6.8	5	8
Japan	9.0	−0.2	4.4	9	135.8	9	2.9	9	9
Philippines	9.2	−7.8	4.0	10	115.2	10	1.8	10	10

One of the factors which we may then evaluate is the level of development of each Asian market compared with the size of its economy. Typically, in a large and developed Western economy such as the United States, the United Kingdom or Germany, the total stockmarket capitalization will average about 50 per cent of the GNP. The reasons for this are logical in that the stockmarket excludes the large part of the economy accounted for by the government or state sector and an equally large part which consists of privately held companies not listed on the public stock exchange. If we assume that the same ratio holds true for Asia (even though the government role in Asian economies tends to be smaller) then it may be of interest to see that some Asian markets are found to be considerably overvalued on this criterion and some which have clearly a great deal of potential for further growth (see Figure 6.3).

There are specific reasons why both Hong Kong and Singapore show a

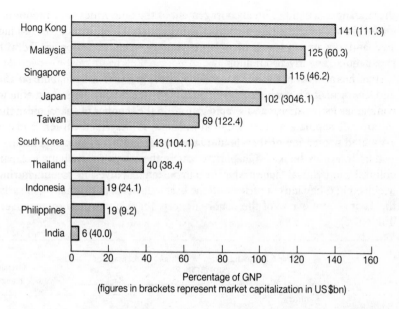

Figure 6.3. Asian stockmarket capitalization as a percentage of GNP, 31 March 1991

ratio of over 100 per cent in market size relative to their GNP. Foreign trade in both these entrepôt states accounts for 200 per cent of GNP and the government is a relatively small player in the economy. Thus even excluding privately held companies the size of the trade, shipping, banking and finance sectors, tends to push up the size of the stockmarket. (On other measures such as price earnings or yield the Hong Kong Market is very undervalued relative to its Asian neighbours.) The Tokyo stockmarket, which had its all time peak in late 1989, reached a ratio of nearly 150 per cent of GNP and was clearly overvalued by any fundamental criterion, including the price earnings ratio which was then at seventy-five times. By March 1991 this figure had fallen back to about 100 per cent but may still be considered expensive compared with the US market which stands at half this level. The real laggards with great growth potential are South Korea, Thailand, Indonesia, the Philippines, India and possibly China.

Nowhere was this case for the catch up effect of a national stockmarket exhibited more clearly than in Indonesia in 1989 when the market rose from 1 per cent of GNP to nearly 20 per cent in two years. This was largely the effect of a change in government fiscal policy to encourage investors to buy shares and entrepreneurs to list their private companies. Many of the large Chinese family companies that had previously remained secretive and closely held, listed their shares and in some cases added US $2–3 billion capitalization to the market overnight. The encouragement of the authorities was, therefore, critical in allowing the capital market to begin to catch up with the economic size and dynamic growth of a large country such as Indonesia with a population of nearly 200 million.

This has also been true in Thailand where the growth has been more steady and less dramatic but where it is still possible to see the regular stream of new companies listing shares and a rapid growth in the number of shareholders in the overall population. The situation in India, as described earlier, is of an estimated population of shareholders now exceeding 10 million.

Earlier in this book in Chapters 4 and 5 there was an evaluation of the cultural and political factors which are important for investors to understand in selecting the Asian countries with the best long-term performance. Clearly the savings rate is one of the major supports for this out-performance (see Table 6.2).

Table 6.2. Savings rates in Asia as a percentage of
GNP/GDP, 1991

Country	%
Singapore	42.8
South Korea	36.2
Japan	33.6
Hong Kong	33.0
Indonesia	31.4
Taiwan	30.8
Malaysia	30.6
Thailand	28.7
India	22.5
Australia	21.1
New Zealand	18.4
Philippines	17.2
United States	15.1

Apart from the underlying rate of savings, another important influence on the level of share prices is the cost of money or the prevailing interest rates in each country. In Table 6.3, there is a snapshot of the interest rates in Asia in 1990. In Table 6.4 interest rates are compared with dividend yields and in Table 6.5 price earnings ratios around Asia are compared. The price to earnings ratio or, when inverted, the earnings yield, does bear a close relation to the cost of money. Japan and Singapore have consistently kept inflation and interest rates relatively low and their equity markets over the long term have commanded higher price earnings multiples as a result. Clearly it can be

Table 6.3. Prime interest rates throughout Asia, June 1991

Country	%
Indonesia	26.0
Philippines	21.0
India	18.0
South Korea	17.5
Thailand	16.0
Australia	14.5
New Zealand	14.0
Taiwan	10.0
Hong Kong	9.5
United States	8.5
Malaysia	8.0
Singapore	7.5
Japan	7.2

Table 6.4. Comparison of Asian interest rates and dividend yields

Country	Prime interest rate (%)	Dividend yield (%)
Indonesia	26.0	3.1
Philippines	21.0	1.6
India	18.0	1.5
South Korea	17.5	1.9
Thailand	16.0	3.8
Australia	14.5	5.7
New Zealand	14.0	5.8
Taiwan	10.0	1.3
Hong Kong	9.5	5.0
Malaysia	8.0	2.7
Singapore	7.5	2.3
Japan	7.2	0.7

argued that Japanese companies have had a competitive advantage in being able to raise capital from the Tokyo stockmarket at such low cost, because of the high multiples and even on convertible bonds, typically a yield of sometimes less than 2 per cent. However, this has begun to change in 1990–1 with the rise in bond yields and the prime rate in Japan.

The high rate of savings mentioned earlier is prevalent throughout the Confucian world (China, Japan, Korea and the overseas Chinese communities). In some countries such as Singapore and Malaysia the rate is artificially boosted by the Central Provident Fund (CPF) scheme, set up by the

Table 6.5. Comparative Asian price earnings ratios,
mid-1991

Country	%
Japan	48.0
Taiwan	39.0
Malaysia	20.9
United States	18.7
Singapore	17.8
South Korea	17.2
Indonesia	16.4
Philippines	15.3
India	15.0
Australia	13.1
Thailand	12.8
Hong Kong	11.0
New Zealand	10.1

Singapore government, which is a form of compulsory savings. However, in Taiwan, Korea and Hong Kong it is much more attributable to the strong sense of family and the desire to provide for education and old age – nations where there is no sickness or unemployment benefit and certainly no old age pensions. It is estimated that the Japanese population as a whole saves more than US $1 billion per day. This is a major source of liquidity to the world's capital markets and has been, for example, channelled into US treasury bonds over the past five years. The comparable savings rate in the United States is around 6 per cent of disposable income compared to an average of nearly 30 per cent in Asia. No single figure can be a more telling indicator of the potential performance of Asian markets compared with Western markets based on this liquidity and, of course, investor confidence.

Clearly the habit of investing in stocks and shares is a relatively new one in Asia. By looking at Table 6.6 and comparing the number of listings and the capitalization of the Asian markets in 1990 with their size in 1981, it is possible to begin to comprehend the phenomenal rate of growth in these markets in the 1980s. Both supply and demand grew rapidly; the number of new listings increased and also the number of investors grew equally, if not more, rapidly. The following table (Table 6.7) gives an idea as to how many shareholders there are in each Asian nation. The Koreans appear to be the most active players of the stockmarket although this may be a misleading ratio in that there are many multi-name accounts in Seoul. More typical of the Chinese communities is the 17 per cent participation of the Hong Kong and Singapore populations in the stockmarket. The stockmarket has, at various times, become something of a cult, for example, most of the sixty-five daily Chinese

Table 6.6. The growth of Asia's emerging markets

	Listings		Market Capitalization (US $ million)	
	1981	1991	1981	1991
South Korea	343	685	4,214	98,200
Taiwan	107	188	5,297	125,500
Hong Kong	204	310	40,700	106,245
Singapore	270	177	34,807	53,864
Malaysia	186	279	15,298	62,100
Philippines	195	155	1,700	8,920
Indonesia	9	129	72	7,010
Thailand	83	232	1,025	31,455
India	2,113	6,000	8,400	40,200
Pakistan	311	505	705	3,200

Table 6.7. Asia's stockmarket investors

	Number of Shareholders (million)	Population (million)	Shareholders as a % of population
South Korea	11.0	42.4	25.9
Singapore	0.47	2.7	17.4
Hong Kong	1.0	5.8	17.2
Taiwan	2.1	20.1	10.4
Japan	10.0	122.8	8.1
Malaysia	1.2	17.4	6.9
India	13.0	818.0	1.6
Philippines	0.65	64.5	1.0
Thailand	0.52	56.2	0.9
Sri Lanka	0.05	16.8	0.2
Indonesia	0.25	182.0	0.1
China	1.0	1,113.0	0.1

newspapers in Hong Kong carry extensive commentaries, recommendations and mathematical analyses on a daily basis. This is even more true in Taipei where taxi drivers, housewives and factory workers all participate in the amazingly active Taipei stockmarket. In fact, the volume of Taiwan shares traded on a daily basis is the third largest in the world after Tokyo and New York and has occasionally even surpassed those markets, despite the fact that there are less than 200 companies listed in Taiwan. The investment game is much less developed in the Philippines, Thailand and the sub-continent (except for India). In China there are estimated to be already 1 million shareholders, mainly in Shanghai, although it should be said that a real share market has not yet developed there.

Monitoring the number of investors in each company is a very good leading indicator of the long-term health and potential of each national market. A market which depends too much on foreign investors, usually a handful of large institutions, is inherently a more volatile and less healthy market than one which depends on a large number of domestic, retail investors. More and more of the de-communizing nations are looking to develop a capital market in order to attract both foreign capital and also the large pools of domestic savings which usually have had no outlet for investment for many years. Hence in Table 6.8 an attempt has been made to speculate on the potential for each of these markets in the next decade.

Table 6.8. Re-emerging markets of the 1990s?

	National	
	Population (million)	GNP (US $ billion)
Shanghai	1,133	415.8
St Petersburg	292	925.6
Saigon	66	11.5
Rangoon	41	8.5
Budapest	11	32.5

RISK IN TERMS OF MARKET VOLATILITY

Table 6.9 compares the rate of volatility in each market with the five-year performance figures. As may be expected the largest and most mature market, namely Japan, produces the lowest volatility rate. However, past performance, both in yen terms and also in US dollars, is correspondingly lower than those of the other Asian countries included in the survey. It is interesting to note, however, that despite its surface political volatility, South Korea has a relatively low market volatility, close to that of Japan. Both Malaysia and Singapore exhibited a higher than expected stability in terms of their index variability. The highest volatility has been experienced in Hong Kong and the smaller South East Asian markets such as Thailand, Indonesia and the Philippines. Table 6.10 studies the specific events which led to this volatility. These cases revolve around the impact on small Asian markets of unexpected external shocks such as the October 1987 global equity crash, or the attempt *coup d'état* in the Philippines, the Tiananmen Square incident on the Hang Seng Index, and so on. This is perhaps the best guide to volatility over a longer period of time when considering that, in the 1990s, even more unexpected political and natural events may strike the Asian markets.

Table 6.9. Comparative volatility rates and performance of Asian markets

Market	Volatility rate	Five-year performance
Japan	0.068	+ 111.04
South Korea	0.083	+ 295.46
Malaysia	0.097	+ 217.78
Singapore	0.098	+ 204.77
Hong Kong	0.100	+ 131.04
Thailand	0.103	+ 588.17
Indonesia	0.112	+ 323.52
Philippines	0.132	+ 394.11
Taiwan	0.183	+ 676.68

Table 6.10. Market volatility rates in periods of greatest turbulence

Market	Time frame	Number of events used in calculation	Volatility rates
Malaysia	30 May 1990–31 Dec. 1990	7	0.060
Singapore	30 Dec. 1988–31 Dec. 1990	24	0.069
South Korea	31 May 1988–31 Dec. 1990	32	0.076
Japan	1 Jan. 1988–31 Dec. 1990	35	0.081
Indonesia	1 Jan. 1990–31 Dec. 1990	11	0.110
Hong Kong	1 Jan. 1980–31 Dec. 1983	47	0.111
Singapore	1 Jan. 1986–30 Nov. 1987	22	0.128
Malaysia	30 April 1986–31 Dec. 1987	20	0.136
Thailand	1 Jan. 1990–31 Dec. 1990	11	0.138
Hong Kong	30 May 1986–31 Dec. 1987	19	0.146
Thailand	1 Jan. 1987–31 Dec. 1987	11	0.147
Hong Kong	1 Jan. 1970–31 Dec. 1974	59	0.169
Taiwan	31 Dec. 1988–31 Dec. 1990	24	0.181
Philippines	1 Jan. 1987–31 Dec. 1987	11	0.188
Singapore	1 Jan. 1981–31 Dec. 1981	11	0.241
Taiwan	31 Dec. 1986–31 Dec. 1987	12	0.251
Singapore	31 Aug. 1972–30 May 1973	7	0.482
Philippines	30 Sep. 1988–30 Sep. 1990	24	0.566

The equation which has been applied to arrive at the volatility rate is as follows:

$$\text{Volatility rate} = \sqrt{\sum_{t=1}^{n} (x - \bar{x})^2 / n}$$

where, $x = 1n$ (index t/index $t-1$); $\bar{x} = \sum x/n$; n = number of events; index t = index of month t; and index $t - 1$ = index of month earlier.

Volatility rate is a convenient measure of market variability. The formula may seem complicated at first but in fact it is quite straightfoward. The term $(x - \bar{x})^2$ simply measures the deviations of individual events from their mean. In addition to making all deviations positive, the squaring also provides mathematical properties that are more desirable for many types of analysis. The summation of the stated terms is then divided by the number of events to obtain the variance. Nevertheless, difficulty arises in interpreting the variance because it is expressed in squared units of measurement. This problem may be circumvented by taking the positive square root of the variance. The resulting term is known as the volatility rate or standard deviation. The higher the volatility rate, the more variability in the market and vice versa.

ASIAN MARKETS DURING PERIODS OF POLITICAL OR ECONOMIC TURBULENCE

In order to illustrate this volatility factor five Asian markets have been examined during six periods of political or economic turbulence and the results are set out in the following sections (see Table 6.11).

Table 6.11. Performance of selective Asian markets

Market	Period	Performance (% change)
Hong Kong	9 March 1973–10 December 1974	− 91.5
Japan	1 October–30 November 1987	− 12.8
Hong Kong	1 May–30 June 1989	− 27.0
Philippines[1]	20 November–18 December 1989	− 30.0
Thailand	1 January–28 February 1991	+ 25.5
Indonesia	1 October 1988–31 December 1989	+202.1

1. High and low of the market for the last two months of 1989

HONG KONG: 9 MARCH 1973 TO 10 DECEMBER 1974

The first modern boom in Hong Kong's share market occurred in 1972. This was five years after the start of the Cultural Revolution in China which had had a profound effect on Hong Kong's confidence. There were riots and serious disturbances in the colony. Property prices plummeted and there was even a question as to whether China would take action to recover the colony from Britain. It became clear, however, that pragmatism would prevail and business went back to normal at the end of the 1960s even though communication and trade with China remained minimal until the late 1970s. Nevertheless, a pattern had been set: the collapse of confidence followed by a strong rebound in share prices, in property prices and general business activity.

Hong Kong, of course, benefited from the strong growth in world trade in the late 1960s and Hong Kong's exports boomed as it was able to supply cheap textiles to the markets of Europe and the United States. At the same time there was a classic 'South Sea bubble' effect caused by taxi drivers, amahs and factory workers buying shares for the first time and during 1972–3 the stockmarket became the main topic of conversation. The boom was abruptly punctured, however, in March 1973 as the index hit a ten-year high of 1774 on 9 March 1973. Within a month it had fallen 50 per cent and from there on it was a long, slow decline to the low of December 1974 when the index reached a low of 150 (see Figure 6.4). Simultaneously the London *Financial Times* Index also hit its all time recent low of about 150. Hong Kong thus reflected the world stockmarket cycle quite accurately. The volatility can also be measured in terms of the turnover which was at its highest just before the peak of the market in March 1973. It took almost ten years before the Hong Kong market recovered a similar level of confidence.

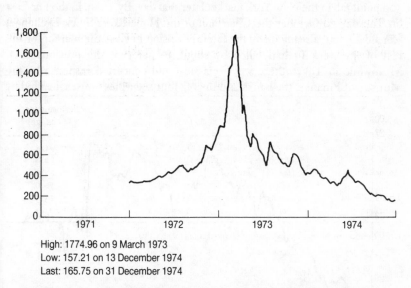

High: 1774.96 on 9 March 1973
Low: 157.21 on 13 December 1974
Last: 165.75 on 31 December 1974

Figure 6.4. Hong Kong Hang Seng price index, from 31 December 1971 to 31 December 1974, actual weekly movements (*Source:* Datastream)

The boom and bust cycle in the Hong Kong equity market is, of course, much shorter than in Western markets, considering that the New York market took almost thirty years to recover the level of 1929. Hong Kong reached a new peak in 1981 and again in 1987. There is every likelihood that it will reach new highs in the six years remaining until the handover to China in 1997. The Hong Kong stockmarket now, in contrast to 1972, is a market dominated by large investors, both large Chinese corporations and London based pension funds, which tends to smooth out some of the more extreme volatility of the earlier years when the market was 90 per cent dominated by small retail investors.

JAPAN: 1 OCTOBER TO 30 NOVEMBER 1987

The October 1987 world stockmarket crash has been studied by many analysts. The immediate causes of the worldwide fall in share prices after a long and extended period of upward movement were complex and varied. Among them was the German decision to raise interest rates at a time when the Federal Reserve was anxious to do the opposite. However, what is clear to the objective observer of this phenomenon of synchronized world share price falls is that the point at which the movement was halted was in Japan. The market fall had started in Hong Kong on Monday morning, 19 October 1987. The European markets were also very weak but the real crunch came with the 500 point fall in the New York market later that day. By 3 a.m. in the Far East on Tuesday 20 October the Chairman of the Hong Kong Stock Exchange, Ronald Li, had already made the fateful decision to close the market for the rest of the week (it had fallen by about 30 per cent the previous day). Meanwhile in Tokyo there was a classical and concerted response by the Ministry of Finance, the banks and the big four securities houses, headed by

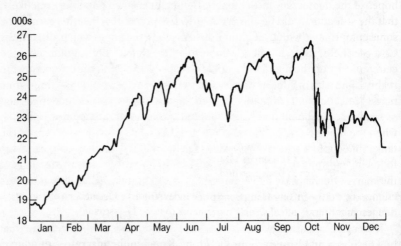

High: 26,646.3 on 14 October 1987
Low: 18,544.00 on 13 January 1987
Last: 21,564.00 on 31 December 1987

Figure 6.5. Japan Nikkei Dow Jones stock average (225) price index from 1 January 1987 to 31 December 1987, actual daily movements (*Source:* Datastream)

Nomura. There was little that they could do immediately on 20 October when the market fell to 22,000, which was, in fact, a fall of less than 15 per cent (and, therefore, considerably less than New York, London or Hong Kong) but by late on 21 October the supporting action had begun and the Tokyo market held steady for the rest of the month with strong buying by Nomura Securities.

What is clear, however, is that this concerted action of confidence in the Far East by the Japanese authorities – and perhaps a genuine reaction by Japan's retail investors believing that their companies were in good health, that Japan's economy was in good shape and that shares were worth buying at such a level – communicated itself fairly quickly to New York, to London and to other world stockmarkets. The buying power was still evident in Japan. The panic subsided within another forty-eight hours. Thus, although markets continued to decline steadily in low volume through November, the worst of the damage was over within the first three days. This action in Tokyo is, therefore, well worth studying for the purposes of future risk assessment and the possible action which authorities can take to support markets in the face of investor panic (see Figure 6.5).

HONG KONG: 1 MAY TO 30 JUNE 1989

In early May 1989 the Hong Kong market was riding high along with the hopes of the democracy movement in Beijing. It seemed possible, even likely, that the students would be allowed to disperse peacefully, that there would be some compromise with the Communist Party and the hopes which all overseas Chinese held, that a liberalization of the system both politically and economically on the mainland would be realized. The first rude awakening to reality came with the declaration of martial law on 19 May and the Hong Kong market fell 300 points immediately. For the next two weeks it traded in a mood of suspended animation between fear and hope, until the night of June 3–4 when the Hong Kong public was able to watch on its television screens as the tanks rolled into Tiananmen Square. The market fell another 500 points the following morning to hit a low of 2,093 (see Figure 6.6). Thus the total fall of the market during May and June was 27 per cent, but the abruptness of the change of policy in China took Hong Kong by surprise and caused a much deeper psychological reaction.

It became apparent within a few weeks after the 4 June incident that business as usual would be the motto of the Chinese government and that although political democracy would be firmly snuffed out, economic reforms might continue. Thus the Hong Kong stockmarket began a long, slow climb back up to 3,000 in 1989–90 during which period it was one of the best performing markets in the world. The pattern of shock, panic and collapse in confidence in June 1989 reflected those of 1972, 1981 and 1987 and was, like those periods, followed by a strong rebound in business confidence during the next two years.

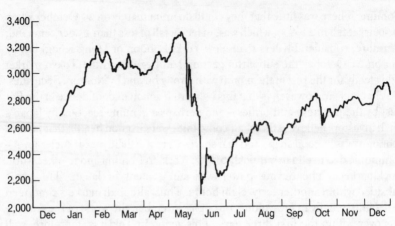

High: 3309.64 on 15 May 1989
Low: 2093.61 on 5 June 1989
Last: 2836.57 on 29 December 1989

Figure 6.6. Hong Kong Hang Seng price index, from 30 December 1988 to 29 December 1989, actual daily movements (*Source:* Datastream)

MANILA: 20 NOVEMBER TO 18 DECEMBER 1989

In 1989 the Philippine stockmarket had recovered its confidence. For the first time since the early months of the Aquino Government in February–June 1986 when the stockmarket had soared on the hopes for the new government, there were signs of strong foreign investor confidence and a more buoyant domestic economy. The Manila stock exchange composite index had risen on the back of these indicators to a new high of 1,300 by late November. The announcement of two overseas mutual funds, the US $50 million Manila Fund in September 1989 and the First Philippine Fund, a US $100 million fund, listed on the New York stock exchange in November 1989, had also boosted confidence. Mrs. Aquino had been to New York and bought the first share of the new fund and it seemed likely that US investors would pour money into the Philippine market. Hence the attempted *coup d'état* of 1 December 1989 rudely shattered those hopes. The Manila market has always traded quite thinly and movements in either direction can be exaggerated. Thus the index fell nearly 20 per cent within the first two or three days of being reopened and there were apparently no buyers (see Figure 6.7). In the six months following the failed coup confidence further evaporated and the index lost more than 50 per cent of its value to reach a low of 600 in the spring of 1990. Just as with Hong Kong in 1989, it took more than eighteen months before confidence had fully returned to the market when it was seen that the Aquino government would survive and a democratic election would proceed normally in 1992.

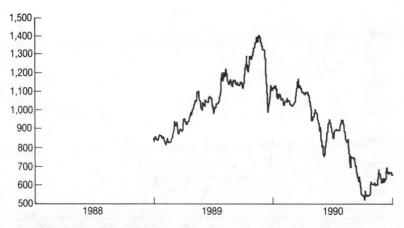

High: 1396.260 on 20 November 1989
Low: 514.800 on 5 October 1990
Last: 651.420 on 31 December 1990

Figure 6.7. Manila stock exchange composite price index, from 30 December 1988 to 31 December 1990, actual daily movements (*Source:* Datastream)

BANGKOK: 1 JANUARY TO 28 FEBRUARY 1991

The successful *coup d'etat* in Bangkok on 23 February 1991 is in marked contrast to the failed attempt in Manila a year earlier and reflected the very different cultural and political traditions of Thailand and the Philippines. In Thailand the coup was bloodless, efficient and supported by the King, the army and a large part of the electorate. It was seen that the ousted prime minister had been guilty of excessive corruption and that the army had a justified cause for complaint. Thus the Bangkok stockmarket, having had a strong rise in the first six weeks of the year, fell 10 per cent overnight and then quickly recovered its nerve as the shape of the new cabinet became clear. The underlying strength of Thailand's economy and market were proven in this test of volatility (see Figure 6.8).

INDONESIA: 1 OCTOBER 1988 TO 31 DECEMBER 1989

The chart of the Indonesian market in 1988–9 looks somewhat similar to that of the new and revived markets of Shanghai, Budapest, Warsaw and other share markets which had had no existence and no volume for a number of years. The jagged movements of the market index reflects a very thin volume and scarcity of listed issues. In October 1988 there were only twenty-four listed companies in Jakarta, of which only eight were available to foreign investors. Total market capitalization was about US $300 million. The announcement of the fiscal

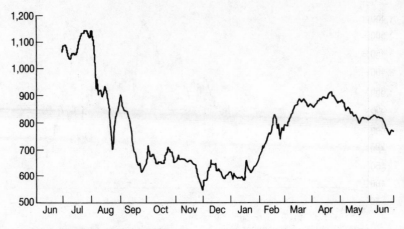

High: 1,143.780 on 25 July 1990
Low: 544.300 on 30 November 1990
Last: 765.210 on 28 June 1991

Figure 6.8. Bangkok stock exchange price index, from 29 June 1990 to 28 June
1991, actual daily movements (*Source:* Datastream)

reforms in October 1988 by the Ministry of Finance and BAPEPAM (the
Capital Markets Executive Agency) provided the initial spark for the market's
rise to 300. This was hardly noticed internationally. However, the launch of
the first Indonesian fund, the Malacca Fund, in January 1989 began to arouse
the interest of foreign fund managers and within six months there were several
imitators. The market continued to trade sideways, however, until August
when it rose 100 per cent in two weeks. Again the volatility of the Indonesian
market was a reflection of the suppy–demand imbalance of share issues
compared with domestic and international demand. Within a year, though,
this supply scarcity had been redressed as the number of listed issues rose to
one hundred and the market began to behave more like other developing
Asian markets with a regular turnover (see Figure 6.9). Such a pattern may
clearly be observed in Shanghai in 1990 and probably will be seen in the other
new stockmarkets in the world in the 1990s.

In order to reduce volatility the classic answer for an investment manager has
been diversification. In Table 6.12 the author has tried to portray, from
personal experience of over ten years in Asia, the best approach to achieving
this stable, long-term growth performance by diversifying among ten different
Asian markets. The actual experience has been that this diversification does
offset volatility and produces superior returns. Typically, during June 1989,
the investment in Thailand was performing so strongly that the sudden

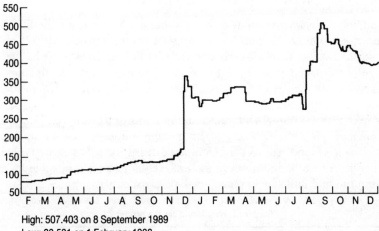

High: 507.403 on 8 September 1989
Low: 83.531 on 1 February 1988
Last : 399.690 on 29 December 1989

Figure 6.9. Jakarta composite price index, from 1 February 1988 to 29 December 1989, actual daily movements (*Source:* Datastream)

Table 6.12. A balanced Asian portfolio

Country	Percentage of portfolio
Japan	20
South Korea	5
Hong Kong	15
India	3
Thailand	20
Taiwan	2
Philippines	5
Indonesia	5
Singapore	10
Malaysia	15

collapse of the Hong Kong market, by 40 per cent in one month, was completely neutralized and the overall portfolio was able to show a 2 per cent growth over the same period. The same has been true of unexpected shocks in the Philippines and even a fall in the Japanese yen. (The rest of the Asian investment zone is basically US dollar linked.)

HOW LIQUID ARE THE MARKETS?

In addition to market volatility an investor has to take account of liquidity in the sense that he or she must be very conscious of the practical difficulties of buying and selling shares in each market. In Table 6.13 an estimate has been made of this factor in terms of the market turnover in each Asian country compared with the size of the market in terms of capitalization. The volatility of each country's monthly turnover has also been estimated. It is surprising to discover that Taiwan, in fact, ranks first in terms of its turnover. However, when measuring the volatility of its monthly turnover a less surprising conclusion is found, namely that the largest market, Japan, has the best overall rating in terms of liquidity. Nevertheless, even in Japan it is possible for an investor to find difficulty in selling medium-sized issues.

Table 6.13. How liquid are the markets?

Market	Average turnover as a % of market capitalization (1981–90)	Rank	Volatility of monthly turnover March 1986– March 1991	Rank	Overall rating
Japan	53.0	3	0.3277	1	1/2
South Korea	56.8	2	0.3874	2	1/2
Taiwan	212.5	1	0.4498	5	3
Thailand	46.1	4	0.4321	4	4
Malaysia	12.3	8	0.4317	3	5
Hong Kong	37.9	5	0.4578	7	6/7
Singapore	34.2	6	0.4528	6	6/7
Philippines	18.8	7	0.5386	9	8
Indonesia	8.2	9	0.5381	8	9

Caution, therefore, is necessary in advising large institutional investors on their Asian portfolios. It is really preferable to take a minimum view of two to five years in order to benefit from the long-term growth of earnings and of share prices, which has characterized the Asian capital markets, and not be exposed to their short-term volatility and liquidity problems. It is also important to note that in many of the smaller markets, such as Thailand and the Philippines, there are both domestic and foreign shares traded. Liquidity in the foreign shares, which often command a premium over the price of domestic shares, is often more restricted. A short-term trading approach simply does not work except possibly in Japan, Hong Kong or Taiwan. Even in these markets an investor in the classic sense of the word usually does better in the long run than the short-term speculator or trader.

7

A FORECAST FOR ASIA
TO THE YEAR 2000

THREE ECONOMIC BLOCS

It is becoming increasingly likely that by the end of the century the world trading system will have coalesced into three major economic blocs. Figure 7.1 and Table 7.1 give a graphical representation of these three blocs and the following text expands further.

Table 7.1. The three economic blocs in the year 2000

	Europe	East Asia	North America
Total GDP[1] (US $ billion)	11,440	11,800	12,950
Total population[1] (million)	575	740	450
Per capita GDP[1] (US $)	19,900	16,000	28,750
Annual real GDP growth 1990–2000	3%	7%	3%

1. Estimated for 2000

BLOC 1: NORTH AMERICA

North America, which includes the United States, Canada and Mexico, is now presently in the process of forming a free trade zone. This North American bloc is likely to be joined during the course of the 1990s by the emerging Latin American bloc which would include all the countries of South America. Brazil, Argentina and Chile are also discussing a free trade zone among themselves and logically all these countries will group together under the leadership of the United States to form a large free trade zone in the western hemisphere.

EUROPE

The growth of the original European Economic Community (EEC – now EC) which consisted of six countries in the 1950s and 1960s – West Germany,

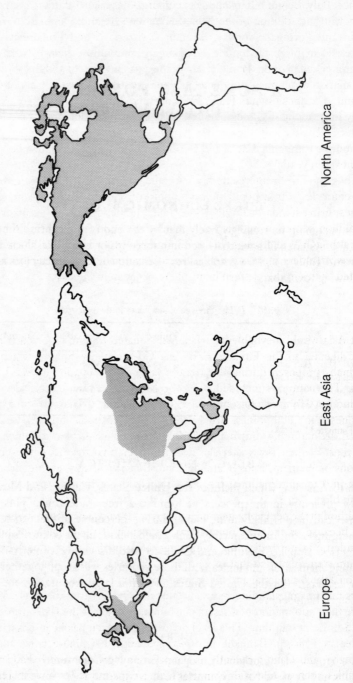

North America

East Asia

Europe

Figure 7.1. The three economic blocs in the year 2000

France, Italy, Belgium, Holland, Luxemburg – has taken off in the last twenty years with the addition of the United Kingdom, Ireland, Denmark, Greece, Spain and Portugal. Norway, Sweden, Switzerland and Finland have all expressed an interest in joining the enlarged Community, as have Turkey and Austria. The fall of the Iron Curtain in the autumn of 1989 and the spread of free market economics and democracy into Eastern Europe has encouraged Poland, Czechoslovakia, Hungary, Romania, Bulgaria and Yugoslavia to apply for eventual EC membership. It is not inconceivable that some of the western republics of the Soviet Union and particulary the three Baltic republics – Lithuania, Latvia and Estonia – would also become members over the next ten years.

Thus, the European free trade zone could eventually include about twenty-five countries with a population of about 500 million, enjoying one of the highest living standards in the world. The reunified nation of Germany with 80 million people, would naturally assume the economic leadership of this bloc although its total weight in the Community would diminish as the number of new members increases and it would have far less dominance than the United States in the western hemisphere or Japan in the east.

EAST ASIA

East Asia would inevitably be a Japan-dominated trading bloc which many have likened to the Greater East Asia Co-prosperity Sphere which was originally proposed during the 1942–5 Japanese occupation of South East Asia. The countries included would be Korea and Taiwan, coastal China, (including Hong Kong and Macau), Thailand, Malaysia, Singapore, Indonesia, the Philippines, Brunei and possibly Australia and New Zealand, which are naturally drawn toward the dynamic Asian bloc to which they sell most of their raw materials. It is also likely that the currently socialist nations of Vietnam, Laos, Cambodia and Burma will also, eventually, come back into the international trading system and gravitate towards this East Asian bloc.

Although the per capita income in this bloc remains lower than in the other two because of the vast populations (especially if the whole of China is included, but not India), the underlying real growth rate, at 7 per cent per annum, remains twice that of Europe or America. Hence, the Asia Pacific region as a commercial and investment opportunity in the next ten or twenty years remains outstandingly attractive for the single reason that there will be more than 500 million new Asian consumers arriving at the take-off point of US $2,000 per annum. This level of affluence, which has been observed in Korea in 1980, in Bangkok in 1990, and even in Chinese cities such as Shanghai and Canton recently, is the point at which demand for consumer durables such as televisions, motorbikes, refrigerators, washing machines, construction materials for houses and even investment and savings products, begins to accelerate towards a critical economic level.

The forecast then for Asia is contained in this simple equation:

population increase × income growth = high economic growth

This is compounded in investment terms by the high savings rates as a proportion of personal income which characterize Asia relative to Western cultures and provide the savings and liquidity for a high rate of capital formation without incurring the levels of sovereign debt or even personal, consumer debt which have characterized Latin America and even the United States. This also means that the high rate of economic growth is not so frequently accompanied by high inflation.

Describing these three economic blocs in the world of 2000 does not imply a growth of protectionism. On the contrary – it is possible to observe a rapid reduction in tariffs and growth of free trade within each bloc but not between the major blocs. For example, the growth in inter-regional trade within Asia during the 1980s has been quite remarkable. Asia's largest export market is Asia. This is a major change. Inter-Asian trade has been growing at a 40 per cent annual rate for the last few years to reach US $300 billion, or more than 10 per cent of the world's total trade. Nearly 20 per cent of ASEAN's US $240 billion annual trade is between these six member countries (Malaysia, Singapore, Thailand, Indonesia, Philippines, Brunei). Another 23 per cent is with Japan and the rest of North East Asia (South Korea and Taiwan). The growth in trade has been accompanied by even more rapid growth in capital investment flows, mainly coming from Japan and its north Asian neighbours and heading south into Thailand, Malaysia, Indonesia and the Philippines. It is estimated that by 2000 if not earlier, more than 50 per cent of Japan's imports will come from Japanese owned factories overseas, mainly located in South East Asia. Producing components at factories in different countries for assembly into a single product is becoming more common. For example, Mitsubishi already exports transmissions from the Philippines, doors from Malaysia and aluminium wheels from Australia to its car plant in Thailand. The rapidly increasing integration of East Asia's manufacturing is a direct outcome of the last decade's liberalization of cross-border flows of capital and goods. Further liberalization will accelerate higher economic growth and larger capital flows within the region. This is also described as the flying geese effect, by which countries with the most advanced technologies hand down their outdated equipment and technologies to those coming up behind them.

ASIA'S MOVE UPMARKET

When the Japanese yen appreciated rapidly against the dollar in 1985–6 textile manufacturers and other Japanese industrialists began to relocate plants in South East Asia. Taiwanese industrialists followed two years later, looking for low labour costs and political stability. The vertical integration of Asian industrial production began to take shape (see Figure 7.2).

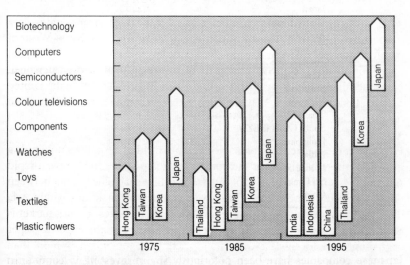

Figure 7.2. Asia's move upmarket

Nowhere is the move upmarket more obvious than in Hong Kong, which has turned itself into a financial and services centre for the region, while moving most of its low labour cost production of toys, shoes and garments into southern China. Will a similar phenomenon be seen in Vietnam? It is difficult to hazard a guess. It is important to recognize the economic and market impact of political changes in communist and decommunized countries. China obviously is going to be a major exporter, although it is going through a two year slowdown at present.

The enormous disparity in labour costs between Japan and China underlines more fully than any other single statistic the potential in the Asian region for this vertical integration of industry implied by a more international division of labour (see Table 7.2). Japan's economic sphere has to expand to enable it to supply its population with low cost consumer goods by producing them in neighbouring low cost Asian nations. Just as the United States will exploit Mexican labour and Western Europe may look increasingly to Eastern and Southern Europe for lower production costs, so Japan has a ready made policy of exporting sunset industries such as textiles, shoes and toys, low cost electronics and assembly plants to its neighbours. Of those neighbours it is likely that China will eventually become the major recipient of Japanese investment although its imports have hardly begun yet since

Table 7.2. Average monthly factory wages, 1990

Country	Average monthly factory wages (US $)
Japan	2,440
United States	2,225
Australia	1,750
Taiwan	700
South Korea	655
Hong Kong	590
Singapore	485
Malaysia	275
Thailand	120
South China (SEZs)	110
Philippines	92
India	60
Indonesia	45
Sri Lanka	40
China	35

Japanese companies have been notoriously shy of investing in communist countries. For the time being, therefore, the major beneficiaries of this outward flow of Japanese capital are still Hong Kong, Singapore, Thailand, the Philippines and Indonesia.

The other sources of capital investment for developing South East Asia are Taiwan, Korea and Hong Kong, as they move up the ladder of value added production and they in turn experience a shortage of cheap labour. This is, therefore, a very healthy process which promotes the prosperity of the region as a whole and brings new employment opportunities to the poorer nations of Asia. Nevertheless, political stability is the *sine qua non* of foreign investment and where it is lacking, for example in the Philippines, foreign investors have been very reluctant to commit long-term investment in manufacturing. Thailand probably receives ten times more Japanese project investments annually than the Philippines although labour costs are broadly similar in the two countries.

DEMOGRAPHICS

Population growth can be considered either as a threat or an opportunity. Clearly there are tremendous pressures on the environment and food resources as the world's population expands from its current 5 billion towards an expected level of around 10 billion by the middle of the next century. Most of this growth will continue to be in Asia, which is likely to reach a total population of 3 billion within the next ten years. Looking at the individual countries, it can be seen that the rate of growth will remain high in some of the smaller countries but that the dominant nations will still be those of China and India. Pressure on urban services will be felt increasingly in cities such as Seoul, Taipei, Bangkok, Manila and Jakarta. Smaller cities such as Kuala Lumpur and Singapore have already put in place the necessary infrastructure in terms of airports, roads, sewage and subway systems, which will allow the expansion of their populations. China is likely to have increasingly serious environmental problems with the rapid spread of industrialization and the shift of population from the countryside to the cities, especially the large, coastal cities such as Shanghai and Canton. Nevertheless, the experience of the past twenty years shows that high economic growth can exceed rapid urban population growth in order to provide for continuously rising living standards in the Asia Pacific region. This is the key to a successful development and investment strategy.

The take-off point of consumption and capital formation has been estimated at US $2,000 per capita. This level in a vast country such as China will only be reached in individual centres such as Shanghai or Canton, as it has been reached in Bangkok, for example, in the late 1980s despite the fact that the Thai peasant population as a whole was still living at an average US $500 per capita. Therefore, national averages may be misleading. The investment opportunity always consists of looking ahead of the present towards the future and seeing how a trend which begins to be apparent in a capital eventually filters down to the surrounding rural populations. On the whole, the free market has done a better job of providing these fast growing Asian populations with the necessary goods and services than the centrally planned economies have done.

THE ENVIRONMENT

Although Asia has lagged behind Europe and North America in its awareness of the ecological risks inherent in economic growth, it is almost certainly true to say that the impact on the world's environment is of a greater magnitude in countries such as China and India than almost anywhere else because of the huge numbers of people and of the rapid pace of industrialization. Air pollution in Peking is worse than that in Los Angeles. The marine life in the Pearl River and around Hong Kong has been almost totally destroyed by factory effluents and unrestricted industrial development in Guangdong Province. Traffic densities in Taipei, Seoul and Bangkok exceed those in London, Paris or New York. Asian people as a whole (although Japan is now an exception to this) are much less environmentally conscious and seem to care less about their environment. The animal wildlife, for instance, has commanded very little respect or attention and forests in Indonesia, the

Philippines and Thailand have been denuded even more rapidly than the highly publicized case of the Amazon. Perhaps the worst case of all and one of the least reported is that of Tibet, where we are reliably informed that the Chinese military have systematically destroyed the fauna, flora and forests of that once beautiful mountain country.

All of this must, however, be seen in perspective. In Table 7.3 a rough estimate has been calculated of the impact per person in the United States (Chicago), Japan (Tokyo) and China (Shanghai) on the consumption of energy, metals and foodstuffs as well as wood resources represented by newsprint. It can, therefore, easily be estimated what impact a doubling in the average living standards in China would have on natural resources in a global context. Certainly there will be renewed upward pressure on the price of oil and other basic minerals if economic growth in China and the Asian region continues in the 1990s at such a rapid pace. Very few countries have estimated the potential of this impact although the influence of China's buying has already been felt on occasions in the rubber market, for example, and even on the London price of copper.

Table 7.3. How much does one person consume?

	Chicago	Tokyo	Shanghai
GNP per capita (US $)	21,118	24,044	310
Primary energy (Tonnes oil equivalent)	7.50	3.10	0.64
Oil (gallons/day)	2.73	1.55	0.80
Copper (kg)	9.00	10.50	0.40
Aluminium (kg)	18.50	13.90	0.70
Raw steel (kg)	400.00	650.00	75.00
Rice (g)	7.00	204.00	351.00
Meat (g)	307.00	69.00	63.00
Sugar (g)	174.00	58.00	12.00
Television sets (per thousand people)	885.00	795.00	8.00
Newsprint (kg)	57.00	28.00	1.30
Newspaper circulation (number of papers/ household)	0.70	1.25	0.25

Source: The Economist – The World in Figures

FORECASTS

In trying to make some forecasts for specific countries of the Asian region it may be as well to consider first the potential negative scenarios, the possible catastrophes, either environmental, economic or political, that could profoundly affect investments in this area of the world. For example, it is a statistical probability that Tokyo will be struck by a major earthquake at some point in the next twenty years and that this will severely affect global financial markets to a degree which was not true during the Great Canto earthquake of 1923. On the other hand, the physical damage to buildings in the greater Tokyo area may, it is predicted, be much less severe than in 1923 when most of the city was built of wood and consequently many more lives were lost in the fire than in the earthquake itself. The breakdown of computer systems in the Tokyo banking and financial markets might have a more severe effect and would, for example, cause immediate falls in share prices in New York and London. However, these are short-term effects which could be remedied.

The recent eruption of two volcanoes, one in Japan and the other in the Philippines, has served as a reminder that this high growth Asia Pacific region is also sitting on the so-called rim of fire which encompasses not only the whole of Japan and the Philippines, but also Indonesia and all the way down to New Zealand. Population increases are also putting a growing pressure on the supply of basic foodstuffs such as rice, which is increasingly grown in a small number of varieties leading to possible greater vulnerability to fungus or pestilence. That and the increased demand for water supply, for instance in the newly industrialized area of southern China, could be the triggers for a severe famine or drought. However, these natural catastrophes are inherently impossible to predict or to provide for and so it is more useful to concentrate on the economic and political events that could cause a surprise.

Among the military conflicts that could erupt in the Asian region in the 1990s, the highest probability must be given to an outbreak of war between North and South Korea. With the death of 79 year old Kim Il Sung the chance of survival of the Pyongyang regime will fall dramatically. The temptation to take military action may, therefore, correspondingly increase. It has been rumoured that the North Koreans now possess an atomic weapon. Certainly the rigid and isolated nature of the North Korean regime makes it less likely to be victim of a sudden internal collapse than was the case in East Germany. There has been no communication – no telephone, no letters, no cross-border travel – between North and South Korea for nearly forty years. The withdrawal of Chinese and Soviet support, both economic and military, for North Korea will also render the country increasingly vulnerable. It appears that North Korea is now seeking economic aid from Japan which has a strategic interest in seeing the continuing division of the peninsula. Certainly a reunified Korea will pose a significant economic challenge to Japan. On the other hand, the reduction in US military commitments around the world will affect its 40,000 ground troops presently stationed in South Korea, and this will also mean a gradual withdrawal from its two major bases in the Philippines.

A new strategic balance in Asia will emerge in the 1990s. To some extent the end of the Cold War and the weakening of both the great powers – the Soviet Union in Siberia and Vietnam, and the United States in Korea, Japan, the Pacific islands and the Philippines – will create a dangerous vacuum which may be filled by China or Japan or small, newly emerging regional powers such as Thailand in the Indochina peninsula. Thus, although the Korean peninsula presents the greatest risk of military conflict it may also present an extraordinary potential for reunification as the example of Germany has already demonstrated. In Table 7.4 it can be seen that the combined population of nearly 65 million and a GNP of US $250 billion does not tell the whole story. The reader must also take into account the extraordinary work ethic of the Korean people and the potential, as West German investment in East Germany has shown, for reconstruction of backward, industrial areas of the former communist country. Both the expanded workforce and the expanded demand for consumer goods would do a great deal to boost the economy of Korea which could well approach its neighbour, Japan, in terms of technology, living standards and share of export markets by the middle of the next century. As previously noted, Korea will also have a lead over Japan in its penetration of the Chinese and Soviet markets. It is, therefore, very well placed, in strategic terms, if it is assumed that the peaceful and positive scenario prevails.

Table 7.4. Economic potential of a unified Korea

	South Korea	North Korea
Population (million)	42.5	22
GDP (US $ billion)	223	35
GDP per capita (US $)	5,230	1,600 (estimate)
Resources	▷ Management and technology ▷ Record export success ▷ Semiconductors, (televisions and videotape recorders) ▷ Automobiles ▷ Steel ▷ Tungsten	▷ Manganese ▷ Coal ▷ Iron ore ▷ Rice/agricultural products

The second area of potential military conflict is across the Formosa Straits. It was only in May 1991 that the Taiwan government finally gave up its government policy of suppressing the communist rebellion and regaining the mainland. The communist Chinese, on the other hand, have not renounced their right to use military force to regain Taiwan. If other methods of persuasion fail it is said that some of the older die-hards in Peking would favour such a policy. However, for the purpose of this study it is assigned a low probability and predicted that there will be a possible *rapprochement* and perhaps reunification of the two Chinas some time before the end of the century, which is sooner than most observers have predicted.

The reasons for this are basically economic. Also there is the important factor of the handover of power in both countries to a younger generation. The people who will rule China and Taiwan in the 1990s will be those who were too young to have experienced the pre-1949 civil war. Instead they will be men and women who are motivated to provide higher economic growth and more jobs and investment to their respective populations. In this context it is interesting to note the tremendous growth in trade and investment between the two major Chinese communities during 1987–91. Trade has now reached over US $4 billion per annum. The number of travellers between the two Chinas now exceeds 1.5 million annually. Investment by Taiwan into China is approaching US $1 billion unofficially and there are thousands of small projects and plans springing up in Xiamen, Shenzhen, Shanghai and all along the coast of mainland China. Top level delegations pass frequently between Taipei and Peking. It is therefore, not entirely fanciful to suppose that the economic integration of what could be called Greater China (see Table 7.5) could lead to an eventual political integration. As China will absorb Hong Kong in 1997 and Macau in 1999 its long-term aim of reunification with Taiwan will become more urgent. The combined GNP of Hong Kong, Macau, Taiwan and China today would exceed US $600 billion and, at present rates of growth, this figure could reach US $2 trillion or very nearly the size of Japan's economy within fifteen years. The magic combination of land, labour and capital which is already fueling the phenomenal growth of the Pearl River estuary, would be even more powerful when expanded to include the whole of southern China.

The third area of potential military conflict is, of course, in the Indochina peninsula where only as recently as the late 1970s it seemed likely that the Pentagon's domino theory of communists toppling country after country in their move south would prevail. However, the southward advance of the communists was held up at the borders of Thailand. It is an historical irony today that it is prosperous and free Thailand which is in turn advancing, in commercial rather than military terms, to dominate the markets of its neighbours – Burma, Laos, Cambodia and Vietnam. Therefore, although it must be considered that there is still a high probability of military conflict, particularly in Cambodia, it seems increasingly likely that the Hanoi government will pay more attention to economic reconstruction than to military adventures. The withdrawal of Soviet economic and military aid will hasten this process and it appears likely that the United States and Vietnam will resume trade and diplomatic relations some time in the early 1990s. This could have quite dramatic consequences for the economy of Vietnam which has been starved of foreign capital and investment. It will in turn spread to Cambodia and Laos, both impoverished, small nations with largely agricultural economies. The Thai businessmen are best placed to take advantage of these new commercial opportunities, as they are on their western

Table 7.5. Greater China

Country	Population (million)	GDP (US $ billion)	Competitive advantages
China	1,125	350.0	Vast resources: land, labour, coal, oil, iron ore, water, agricultural products, satellite launching and nuclear technology.
Taiwan	20.7	171.1	US $60 billion reserves Vigorous export economy Semiconductor technology US-educated entrepreneurs and PhDs
Hong Kong (1 July 1997)	5.8	70.8	Deepwater port and number one container terminal (annual throughput 25 million tonnes) Infrastructure: finance, telecommunications, MTR, shipping, tourism and legal system China re-exports
Macau (20 December 1999)	0.45	3.7(E)	Textile quotas Infrastructure Tourism
	1,151.95	595.6	

border with the Burmese. As the Burmese way of socialism sputters out to its inglorious end, it is, once again, Thai companies and Thai smugglers who will exploit the situation.

Again, military conflict is very possible in the struggle for control of Burma, a once prosperous country with valuable oil and mineral reserves. Burma, like Thailand, remains largely Buddhist. However, it is likely to be the minorities such as the Karen and other tribes in the Golden Triangle who would be the immediate cause of the insurrection or guerilla warfare.

Looking at the population statistics in the Indochina peninsula (see Table 7.6) it can be seen that it is Vietnam, with its population approaching 70 million, which is likely to provide the competition in the 1990s for Thailand's textile and other export industries. The Vietnamese are a hardworking, disciplined people and the former south Vietnamese, in particular centred around Saigon, have had a mere fifteen years under the impoverished rule of the northern communists and will, therefore, revert quite quickly to the market oriented mentality of pre-1975 times.

Thailand's role in the Indochina peninsula is highlighted not only in economic and commercial terms but also in military terms. A strong economy implies a strong military as Japan has also discovered despite its pacifist constitution. The Thai military has good morale, good equipment and plays an important political role in the country. Looking at the history of the last few

Table 7.6. Thailand and the domino theory in reverse

Country	Population (million)	GNP US $ billion	Per capita GNP (US $)
Thailand	56.2	72.3	1,286
Vietnam	66	11.5	175
Burma	40	8.0	200
Cambodia	8	0.9	110
Laos	4	0.68	170

centuries in this area it can be seen that it is likely that Thailand will regain some of its territories lost in the nineteenth century to the encroachments of the former French and British empires.

Other potential military conflicts that could affect investors in Asia are really confined to the Philippines where a communist insurgency continues in a faltering manner. The financial assistance which the Filipino communists have received in the past from China and other communist nations is likely to be reduced. Similarly, the Muslim insurgents in the south are being increasingly isolated and their only supporter in the past appears to have been Quathafi of Libya. It is, therefore, not too optimistic to predict that the Philippine government can regain control over the whole archipelago in a short time. Popular support for the rebels is very limited and the survival of the democratic process in the Philippines will be confirmed by the elections of 1992 and give greater legitimacy to the elected government.

One strategic area which has not been much discussed by economic or military analysts is the area of central Asia where the two empires of China and the Soviet Union meet. In the past this has always been a turbulent and restless area because of the ethnic diversity of the various peoples – Kazakhs, Tajiks and Uzbeks on the Russian side, and Uighurs, Tibetans and Mongolians on the Chinese side. The reason that this area may come into sharp focus by the year 2000 or later is the recent report that a very large oilfield has been found in the Tarim Basin in central Sinkiang. Oil industry analysts expect that it will be a minimum of fifteen years, say by 2005 to 2010, before this oil can be fully explored, drilled and extracted by pipeline to the nearest coastline over 3,000 miles away. The enormous practical difficulties of exploiting this valuable energy reserve, however, will not prevent a possible political struggle to control it. However, it is likely that China's determination to maintain its western borders (shown in the ruthless supression of any opposition to its rule in Tibet) will prevail and that Sinkiang will become an increasingly valuable province to China.

THE INFLUENCE OF THE OVERSEAS CHINESE
ON THE WEST

There are four main areas where the new wave of Chinese immigrants in the 1980s will begin to have an important impact by the end of this century – Canada, Australia, the west coast of the United States (California) and the United Kingdom.

CANADA

More than 50 per cent of the skilled emigrants from Hong Kong in the 1980s have obtained Canadian passports and, of these, the destinations they have chosen have been split equally between Vancouver and Toronto. While Toronto is a much larger and more ethnically diversified city, with its important financial markets and its close link to US trade and investment across Lake Ontario – it is, in fact, the established centre of British Canada – it is easier for an analyst to see the impact of the new Chinese communities of Canada in the fast growing, western city of Vancouver – the main commercial and financial centre of British Columbia. Here it is estimated that the Chinese community coming mainly from Hong Kong but also Taiwan, comprises nearly 20 per cent of the total urban population of 1.5 million.

The impact of these new immigrants (often called the 'yacht people' to distinguish them from the boat people, since they are wealthy, educated and often retired entrepreneurs from Hong Kong) is very visible not least in the rise in real estate values during the last ten years in Vancouver. Essentially the government of British Columbia took a courageous view in the late 1970s when unemployment in the province was nearly 15 per cent and there was a desperate need to create new employment opportunities and attract new capital. Much of the province's economy was still dependent on the timber and pulp industry. Nevertheless, British Columbia has a very attractive climate, a much warmer winter than the rest of Canada and attractive natural parks and ski resorts for development of the tourism industry. Hong Kong Chinese people were able to obtain a Canadian passport with around C $150,000 and less stringent residency qualifications than in the United States.

The largest and most visible investment made by any Hong Kong Chinese entrepreneur was made by Mr Li Ka Shing of Cheung Kong and Hutchison, who has made a commitment to build a C $3 billion development of offices and apartments on the Expo Canada site adjoining the central business district. Many other downtown buildings have been similarly purchased by wealthy investors from Hong Kong. Most symbolic of the new Chinese presence was the appointment as Lieutenant Governor of Dr David Lam who combines his civic duties with a philanthropy based on the fortune he has made from real estate development in Vancouver during the past twenty-five years. Even in the United States his appointment would be exceptional in giving a first generation immigrant the opportunity to occupy such an exalted and influential position. He is spoken of with great respect and affection by Canadians of every background.

Hence, in Vancouver, it is possible to see a very positive impact from the new Chinese communities and the gradual transformation of a group of wealthy refugees into a group of concerned and contributing citizens in their new country. There is no doubt that Canada as a whole will benefit greatly from the skills and investment and new ideas which this group will bring and, over the long term, from the links which their families will build between Canada, Hong Kong and China.

AUSTRALIA

At first sight China and Australia have little in common, except an accident of geography which placed the emptiest continent directly south of the world's most populous nation. There is obviously a complementary relationship in the vast natural resources of Australia and the vast human resources of its northern neighbour.

In the two hundred or so years since the first fleet of convict ships sailed into Sydney harbour in 1788, no group of immigrants into Australia has looked in any way like the Hong Kong Chinese arriving every morning on the overnight Qantas and Cathay flights from Hong Kong. Sydney airport is a sea of Asian faces. Many of them are husbands and fathers who have brought their wives and children down to Australia, bought houses in Sydney and commute back and forth to Hong Kong where they still run businesses. They are called the 'astronauts' because they shuttle up and down between the two places.

However, there is a wide diversity in the 200,000 or so Chinese who live in Australia, some recent arrivals and some who have been in Australia for more than a generation. As in Canada, there has been a gradual shift from purely business activity to adopting a higher profile and taking a tentative role in the political life of the community. For example, in Sydney, the first Asian parliamentarian in Australia is Mrs Helen Sham Ho who is a Liberal party member of the New South Wales legislature. Like David Lam in Canada, she came down from Hong Kong thirty years ago and is an active representative of the Chinese community in Sydney. It will be recalled that Australia maintained its white Australian policy as recently as 1970, and thus it is impressive to see the rapid growth and growing influence of the new ethnic communities in Australia. There are also many Chinese doctors, accountants and lawyers who have brought their skills 'down under'. Relatively few, in fact, can be classified as the 'astronauts' shuttling between Hong Kong and Sydney. As 1997 approaches even these people will be forced to make a commitment.

Although the Australian economy has been rather depressed during the past two to three years (and this has caused some waiverers to return to Hong Kong and its more active business opportunities), the majority of the Chinese community in Australia take a longer-term view and see the country as being stable and offering a pleasant lifestyle and good education for their children. At the end of the 1980s Australia was absorbing about 10,000 Chinese immigrants a year from Hong Kong, Taiwan, Macau and China. This may well slow down owing to economic pressures. (The situation is parallel in Canada which may also tighten up controls on immigration in the early 1990s.) There is, of course, some opposition to the rapid immigration of the 1980s. One spokesman for this group in Australia is the historian, Professor Geoffrey Blayney, who argues that fundamentally and culturally, a pluralistic society cannot absorb so many people from a different linguistic and cultural background so well, with over 50 per cent of Australia's immigrants coming from Asia in the past ten years.

However, nobody in Australia can disagree with the view that the country has no choice in the future but to tie itself more closely with Asia, in terms of trade and investment, and that this will inevitably mean a greater movement of people in both directions. The former Prime Minister, Malcolm Fraser, takes a long-term view of this situation. Australia really lost its close ties with Britain twenty years ago when the United Kingdom joined the EC. Australia's biggest trading partner has been and continues to be Japan. However, most of its agricultural and mineral exports – wool, coal, meat and so on – will also find new and expanding markets in Korea, Taiwan and China. Fraser believes that Australia and New Zealand must join the major Asian nations in forming a Pacific Trade Association. If this basic change of focus really takes root in Australian business, education and political life, it will have a very beneficial impact on Australia's future, since its economy increasingly will be tied in with the dynamic Asian region. My forecast is, therefore, that the Chinese will play an important, but minor, role in the future life of Australia and that Australia will be increasingly the destination for investment, for immigration, for tourism and for trade with the Asian region, especially Japan.

THE WEST COAST OF THE UNITED STATES (CALIFORNIA)

San Francisco was known among the Chinese in the nineteenth century as the 'golden mountain' since the start of Chinese immigration there coincided with the Gold Rush of 1849. From this time onwards a small Chinese community has existed on the west coast. In more recent years this has grown dramatically beyond San Francisco to include Los Angeles and other Californian cities. It is part of an overall change in the pattern of US immigration, away from Europe towards South America and Asia. There are now estimated to be nearly 10 million Asians, or more than 3 per cent of the US population, mainly centred on the west coast. It is, therefore, difficult to assess the impact of the recent wave of immigrants from Hong Kong and from China since they have been absorbed in the already large west coast Chinese community. One area where they are very visible is on the campuses of major universities such as Berkeley, outside of San Francisco. Here the main issue has been the application of quotas to ethnic groups in awarding places in universities. The undoubted academic success of the Asian Americans has led to a backlash from other ethnic groups. None the less, this overachievement is the result of hard work and study, especially on the part of those who have recently arrived in the United States. For example, a very large percentage of the students sent from China to study in US universities have elected to stay on following the June 1989 events in Peking. Some of these students are outstanding scientists and will make a significant contribution to American academic and scientific life in the future.

Like Canada, the USA has benefited from a steady inflow of capital from Asia, led by Japan but also including wealthy Chinese families from Hong Kong, Taiwan, Singapore, Malaysia, Indonesia, Thailand and the Philippines. Much of this investment is concentrated in real estate, again mainly on the west coast but also in areas such as Texas and New York. There have also been notable cases of corporate investment and takeovers. For example, the Hong Kong group, New World, purchased the US hotel chain, Ramada Inn, and the Thai group, Unicord, purchased Bumble Bee, a distributor of food products in the United States, in takeovers worth more than US $500 million each. This is probably only the beginning of a wave of major investments in the United States which will continue in the 1990s. Given the enormous size of the US economy these investments have only a very marginal impact and are much less visible than, for instance, the Japanese purchase of major buildings in downtown New York and Los Angeles or of major US companies. Nevertheless, there is an undoubted benefit to the USA in the commitment of these new immigrants and the investment by Asian companies and individuals who have a continuing interest and stake in the United States.

THE UNITED KINGDOM

In late September 1990 the UK government finally granted 50,000 Hong Kong Chinese families the chance to obtain a British passport and residency. Unlike the examples of Canada, Australia and the United States, Britain did not insist on these families moving to Britain. It was, instead, a form of insurance policy intended to allay the fears of leading Hong Kong people after Tiananmen Square. It was deliberately designed to attract young, professional families with qualifications, a good knowledge of the English language and some ties with Britain, whether through schooling or family. In the event, the response has been disappointing but it has done something to further cement the long-standing ties between Hong Kong and Britain where well over 100,000 Chinese people are living. For many years families from the New Territories of Hong Kong have emigrated under a special scheme to settle in many parts of the United Kingdom especially the Midlands. Many students from Hong Kong attend universities in Britain.

Although knowledge of the English language among Hong Kong school children and university students is probably not as high in the 1990s as it was twenty years ago, owing to the lack of native language teachers and the gradual feeling that it may be as useful in the future to speak Mandarin Chinese, the Hong Kong–United Kingdom link will remain after 1997. London, like Vancouver and Sydney, has benefited from a small wave of property investment from Hong Kong families. The ability to gain entry to the European Community and to be able to reside anywhere in the twelve member countries is an attraction to Hong Kong people gaining UK passports, as it is also to Macau residents taking up Portuguese passports. It is, however, disappointing to realize how few people in Britain understand the significance of Hong Kong and how few British businesspeople appreciate the commercial potential of the British position in China both before and after 1997. There is still a great deal of goodwill and there are still strong links to be built up.

Hong Kong is becoming increasingly an international centre where Japanese or French or American companies will have just as strong a position as British companies when approaching the Chinese market. It would not be too fanciful to predict that the Chinese impact on Britain, and thence on Europe, will grow steadily in the next ten to twenty years. It will be just as much an impact on investment and trade as it will be a cultural impact. Even after Britain's link with Hong Kong has ended, the flow of people and ideas and trade between the two countries will be maintained.

A SURE FORECAST

At midnight on 30 June 1997, the Union flag will be pulled down its flagpole at Government House in Hong Kong. Two years later the Portuguese will leave Macau. This will end several centuries of European presence and colonization in East Asia. The Chinese will again control China, pending the return to the fold of Taiwan.

So it appears – but appearances, especially in the Chinese world, can be deceptive. The Western influence will linger. Western ideas have been absorbed into business, science, medicine, law and government; older Chinese ideas, especially in medicine and law, are still very strong and may prove most lasting in this part of the world. None the less, the symbolic date of 1997 represents an important turning point.

For the past two centuries (since perhaps the first British embassy to the

Emperor Chien Lung in 1793) the insistent pressure, in terms of trade, technology and ideas, has been from West to East. In the twenty-first century the tide will be reversed. The pressure and the expansion will come from the East. It will most likely be a peaceful pressure but it is certain that the economic dynamism of Asia will increasingly spill out, in a myriad of ways, over the Occidental world.

BIBLIOGRAPHY

Adshead, S. A. M. (1988) *China in World History*, USA: St Martin.

Aikman, David (1986) *Pacific Rim: Area of change, area of opportunity*, USA: Little.

Armour, Andrew (1985) *Asia and Japan, The search for modernisation and identity*, USA: Humanities.

Baker, Hugh D. R. (1979) *Chinese Family and Kinship*, New York: Columbia University Press.

Barr, Pat (1967) *The Coming of the Barbarians*, London: Macmillan.

Barr, Pat (1968) *The Deer Cry Pavilion*, London: Macmillan.

Beasley, W. G. (1963) *The Modern History of Japan*, London: Weidenfeld & Nicolson.

Benedict, Ruth (1946) *The Chrysanthemum and the Sword*, Japan: Charles E. Tuttle.

Bird, Isabella (1985) *Korea and her Neighbours*, USA: Routledge Chapman & Hall.

Bloodworth, Dennis (1986) *The Tiger and the Trojan Horse*, Singapore: Times Books International.

Blunden and Elvin (1983) *Cultural Atlas of China*, Oxford: Phaidon Press.

Bonavia, David (1989) *The Chinese*, Harmondsworth: Penguin.

Bond, Michael Harris (1986) *The Psychology of the Chinese People*, New York: Oxford University Press.

Braudel, Fernand (1972) *The Mediterranean in the Age of Philip II*, London: Harper & Row.

Braudel, Fernand (1984) *Civilisation and Capitalism 15th–18th Century, Vol. 3, The Perspective of the World*, London: Collins.

Brosseau, Maurice (1991) *China Review* (ed. Kuan Hsin-chi), Hong Kong: The Chinese University Press.

Butterfield, Fox (1983) *China, Alive in the Bitter Sea*, UK: Coronet.

Calder, Kent E. (1988) *Crisis and Compensation: Public policy and political stability in Japan 1949–1986*, New Jersey: Princeton University Press.

Calverley, John (1990) *Country Risk Analysis* (second edition), London: Butterworth.

Ching, Frank (1988) *Ancestors*, New York: William Morrow.

Chula Chakrabongse, Prince (1960) *Lords of Life: A history of the kings of Thailand*; London: Alvin Redman.

Clayre, Alistair (1984) *The Heart of the Dragon*, Glasgow: Collins.

Cleary, J. C. (ed.) (1991) *Worldly Wisdom: Confucian teachings of the Ming Dynasty*, UK and USA: Shambhala Publications.

136 Bibliography

Coedes, G. (1966) *The Making of South East Asia*, London: University of California Press.
Cooper, J. C. (1981) *Yin and Yang*, England: Thorsons.
Cronin, Vincent (1955) *The Wise Man from the West*, London: Rupert Hart-Davis.
Economic Planning Agency (1983) *Japan in the Year 2000*, Tokyo: The Japan Times Ltd.
Economist, The (1988) *Directory of World Stock Exchanges*, USA: Johns Hopkins.
Elvin, Mark (1973) *The Pattern of the Chinese Past*, California: Stanford University Press.
Fairbank, John K., Edwin O. Reischauer and Albert M. Craig (1973) *East Asia: Tradition and transformation* (Modern Asia edition), Japan: Houghton Mifflin.
Fairbank, John K. and Edwin O. Reischauer (1978) *China, Tradition and Transformation*, USA: Houghton Mifflin.
Far East Economic Review (1984–87) *Asia Year Books*, Hong Kong.
Feis, Herbert (1953) *The China Tangle*, New Jersey: Princeton University Press.
Fitzgerald, C. P. (1935) *China: A short cultural history*, London: Barrie & Jenkins.
Fraser, John (1980) *The Chinese: Portrait of a people*, USA: Summit Books.
Gibney, Frank (1979) *Japan, The Fragile Superpower*, New York: New American Library.
Goldberg, Michael (1985) *The Chinese Connection*, Canada: University of British Columbia Press.
Gungwu, Wang (1991) *China and the Chinese Overseas*, Singapore: Times Academic Press.
Halberstam, David (1987) *The Reckoning*, London: Bloomsbury.
Hall, D. G. E. (1955) *A History of South East Asia*, London: Macmillan Education.
Hicks, George (1989) *Hong Kong Countdown*, Hong Kong: Writers' & Publishers' Cooperative.
Hicks, George (ed.) (1990) *The Broken Mirror: China after Tiananmen*, London: Longman.
Hofheinz and Calder (1983) *The Eastasia Edge*, USA: Basic.
Homer, Sidney (1987) *A History of Interest Rates* (second edition), New Brunswick & London: Rutgers University Press.
Hong Kong Government (1985–90) *Hong Kong Yearbooks (1985–90)*.
Hsu, I. (1970) *The Rise of Modern China*, New York: Oxford University Press.
Ishihara (1991) *The Japan That Can Say No*, London: Simon & Schuster.
Kennedy, Paul (1989) *The Rise and Fall of the Great Powers*, USA: Random House.
Keswick, Maggie (ed.) (1982) *The Thistle and the Jade*, London: Octopus Books.
Kotkin and Kishimoto (1988) *The Third Century*, USA: Crown.
Latourette (1934) *The Chinese: Their history and culture*, New York: Macmillan.
Lloyd George, Robert (1989) *A Guide to Asian Stock Markets*, Hong Kong: Longman Group (Far East).
Longman (1975) *The China Investment Guide*, Hong Kong.
Longman and China Statistical Information Consultancy (1986) *Statistical Year Book of China 1987*, Hong Kong.
McGurn, William (1988) *Basic Law, Basic Questions*, Hong Kong: Review Publishing.
MacIntyre, Michael (1985) *The New Pacific*, London: Collins.

Mackay, Charles (1841) *Extraordinary Popular Delusions and the Madness of Crowds*, London: Richard Bentley.

MacLeod, Roderick (1988) *China Inc: How to do business with the Chinese*, USA & UK: Bantam Books.

Macrae, Norman (1984) *The 2024 Report*, London: Sidgwick & Jackson.

Maraini, Fosco (1960) *Meeting with Japan*, New York: Viking Press.

Merson, John (1989) *Roads to Xanadu*, London: Weidenfeld & Nicolson.

Michener, James (1959) *Hawaii*, New York: Random House.

Morita, Akio and Sony (1987) *Made in Japan*, London: Fontana Collins.

Morris, Jan (1988) *Hong Kong*, London: Viking.

Needham, Joseph and Ronan, Colin (1978, 1981, 1986) *Science and Civilisation in China*, Vols. I–III, Cambridge: Cambridge University Press.

Norman, Henry (1892) *The Real Japan*, London: T. Fisher Unwin.

Norman, Henry (1895) *The Far East*, London: T. Fisher Unwin.

Norman, Henry (1895) *The People and Politics of the Far East*, London.

Packard, Jerrold, M. (1988) *Sons of Heaven: Portrait of the Japanese Monarchy*, London: Queen Anne Press.

Pan, Lynn (1990) *Sons of the Yellow Emperor*, London: Secker & Warburg.

Patrikeeff, Felix (1989) *Mouldering Pearl: Hong Kong at the Crossroads*, London: George Philip Ltd.

Peh-T'i-Wei, Betty (1987) *Shanghai: Cricible of Modern China*, USA: Oxford University Press.

Pomfret, Richard (1991) *Investing in China*, Hemel Hempstead: Harvester Wheatsheaf.

Polo, Marco (1908) *Travels*, London: Dent.

Redding, S. Gordon (1990) *The Spirit of Chinese Capitalism*, Berlin: Walter de Gruyter.

Reischauer and Craig (1979) *Japan, Tradition and Transformation*, Australia: George Allen & Unwin.

Rodwell, Sally (1991) *A Visitor's Guide to Historic Hong Kong*, Hong Kong: The Guidebook Company.

Robert, J. M. (1976) *A History of the World*, London: Hutchinson.

Rowley, Anthony (1987) *Asian Stock Markets: The inside story*, Hong Kong: Far Eastern Economic Review.

Sansom, George (1958) *A History of Japan* (3 vols), UK: Dawson.

Seagrave, Sterling (1985) *The Soong Dynasty*, London: Sidgwick & Jackson.

Seeley, Sir John, 'The Expansion of England', Lecture 1.

Spence, Jonathan D. (1974) *Emperor of China*, New York: Alfred A. Knopf.

Snow, C. P. (1966) *Variety of Men*, London: Macmillan.

Snow, Edgar (1968) *Red Star Over China*, London: Victor Gollancz.

Snow, Philip (1988) *The Star Raft*, London: Weidenfeld & Nicolson.

Statler, Oliver (1961) *Japanese Inn*, London: Secker & Warburg.

Statler, Oliver (1983) *Japanese Pilgrimage*, New York: William Morrow.

Swee-Hock, Saw (1989) *Investment Management in Singapore*, Singapore: Longman Singapore Publishers and the Stock Exchange of Singapore.

Tasker, Peter (1987) *Inside Japan*, London: Sidgwick & Jackson.

Temple, Robert K. G. (1986) *China, Land of Discovery and Invention*, UK: Patrick Stephens.

138 Bibliography

Templeton, John (1987) *The Templeton Plan: 21 principles of success and happiness*, New York: Harper Row.

Thubron, Colin (1987) *Behind the Wall*, London: Heinemann.

Turnbull, Mary (1980) *A Short History of Malaysia, Singapore and Brunei*, Singapore: Graham Brash.

Tzu, Sun (1971) *The Art of War*, USA: Oxford University Press.

Vare, Daniele (1939) *The Temple of Costly Experience*, London: Methuen.

Vare, Daniele (1988) (first published 1939)*The Maker of Heavenly Trousers*, UK: Black Swan.

Viner, Aron (1987) *Inside Japan's Financial Markets*, London & Japan: The Economist Publications.

Viner, Aron (1988) *The Emerging Power of Japanese Money*, Tokyo: The Japan Times Ltd.

Waley, Arthur (1958) *The Opium War through Chinese Eyes*, California: Stanford University Press.

Waley, Arthur (1941) *Translations from the Chinese*, Indiana: Alfred A. Knopf Inc.

Wilson, Dick (1970) *Asia Awakes*, London: Weidenfeld & Nicolson.

Wilson, Dick (1984) *Chou*, London: Hutchinson.

Wilson, Dick (1990) *Hong Kong, Hong Kong*, London: Unwin Hyman.

Winchester, Simon (1988) *Korea*, Englewood Cliffs: Prentice Hall.

Winchester, Simon (1991) *The Pacific*, London: Hutchinson.

Wright and Pauli (1987) *The Second Wave*, London: Waterlow.

Yutang, Lin (1937) *The Importance of Living*, New York: John Day.

Yutang, Lin (ed.) (1942) *The Wisdom of China and India*, New York: Random House.

Yuan, D. Y. (1988) *Chinese–American Population*, Hong Kong: UEA Press.

Zengage, Thomas and Tait Ratcliffe (1988) *The Japanese Century, Challenge and Response*, Hong Kong: Longman.

INDEX

Asia,
  future strategic balance, 123–4
Association of South East Asian Nations
  (ASEAN), 118
Australia,
  in Asia–Pacific region,
    and immigraiton from China, 129–30
    and integrated industrial production, 120
    trade,
      East Asia bloc, 117
      with Japan, 64

banking,
  in Hong Kong, 59
  and risk analysis, 41–2
Brunei,
  trade, East Asia bloc, 117–18
Burma, 125–7
  contrasted with Thailand, 77
  trade, East Asia bloc, 117

Cambodia,
  trade, East Asia bloc, 117
Canada, 21–2, 128–9
China, People's Republic of,
  in Asia–Pacific region,
    and Hong Kong, 59, 60, 106, 109
    and integrated industrial production,
      119–20
    and Taiwan, 54, 67–70, 124–5, 126
  economy,
    consumption per person in Shanghai,
      122
    exchange rate, 56
    and history, 9–10
    inflation, 41, 56
    investment considerations, 51–3
    performance, 49
  environment, 121
  and foreign powers, 50–1
  history, 3–5, 7–10, 13–19, 28–9

economic and technological progress,
  1–3
trends, 53–4
and Islam, 6
migration from 15–22
  maps, 18, 20
  migrants' origins, 15–17
  to Australia, 129–30
  to Canada, 21–2, 128–9
  to United Kingdom, 131–2
  to United States, 19, 21, 130–1
oil, 127
people, prospects, 25–7
population, 121
special economic zones, 51
trade,
  East Asia bloc, 117
  foreign, 56–7
  see also stockmarkets
Chinese,
  language, 13
  people, as business community in
    Indonesia, 86–7
currency
  Chinese renmimbi/yuan, 56
  Filipino peso, 91
  Hong Kong dollar, 61
  Indonesian rupiah, 87
  Japanese yen, 65
  Korean won, 74
  Malaysian ringgit, 81–2
  Thai baht, 78–9

democracy, 33–4

East Asia,
  trade bloc, 116, 117–18
environment, 121–2
Europe,
  economic and technological progress, 1–3